Collaborative Advantage

Collaborative Advantage

Winning Through
Extended Enterprise Supplier Networks

Jeffrey H. Dyer

OXFORD
UNIVERSITY PRESS
2000

OXFORD
UNIVERSITY PRESS

Oxford   New York
Athens   Auckland   Bangkok   Bogotá   Buenos Aires
Calcutta   Cape Town   Chennai   Dar es Salaam   Delhi
Florence   Hong Kong   Istanbul   Karachi   Kuala Lumpur
Madrid   Melbourne   Mexico City   Mumbai   Nairobi
Paris   São Paulo   Singapore   Taipei   Tokyo   Toronto   Warsaw

and associated companies in
Berlin   Ibadan

Copyright © 2000 by Oxford University Press

Published by Oxford University Press, Inc.
198 Madison Avenue, New York, New York 10016

Library of Congress Cataloging-in-Publication Data

Dyer, Jeffrey H.
Collaborative advantage :
winning through extended enterprise supplier networks / Jeffrey H. Dyer
p.   cm.
Includes bibliographical references and index.
ISBN 0-19-513068-5
1. Chrysler Corporation—Management. 2. Toyota Jidasha Kagya Kabushiki Kaisa—Management.
3. Industrial procurement—Case studies. 4. Business networks—Case studies.
5. Comparative management. I. Title.

HD9710.U54 C454 2000
658.7′2—dc21
00-041643

1 3 5 7 9 8 6 4 2
Printed in the United States of America
on acid-free paper

Contents

Preface

In this book I make the case that future competitive advantage will be created by teams of companies rather than by single firms. Competition between single firms, while perhaps still the rule, is becoming less universal as networks of allied firms have begun to compete against each other. Competitive advantage is increasingly jointly created, and shared, by teams of firms within a value chain. This is what I refer to as *collaborative advantage* within the extended enterprise. (The term *extended enterprise* refers to a value chain in which the key players have created a set of collaboration processes that allow them to achieve virtual integration and work together as an integrated team.) Toyota and Chrysler have achieved staggering performance advantages relative to their major competitors (e.g., General Motors, Ford, Nissan) during the past decade in large part because they have created more effective extended enterprises.

The winners of the next decade and beyond will understand how to create collaborative advantage. They will understand the key trends that continue to push firms to both focus on an ever narrower set of core competencies and develop closer partnerships with other firms in their value chain. They will recognize where and when to make investments in dedicated assets in order to optimize the value chain in which they are embedded. They will develop routines for sharing knowledge with their partners in the extended enterprise, thereby enhancing the competencies of all enterprise members. They will know how to develop trust with those partners so that the extended enterprise can swiftly and flexibly respond to opportunities and threats while maintaining very low transaction costs. And they will also understand that strategy is no longer an individual firm phenomenon but will increasingly be done in concert with a firm's partners in the extended enterprise. In this book I will demonstrate the power of collaborative advantage by showing that Toyota, during the 1980s and 1990s, and Chrysler, during the 1990s, have been the highest performing automakers (with twice the profits of key competitors) largely because they have organized and managed their supply chain networks more effectively than competitors.

The book had its origins in the spring of 1985. I was a freshly minted M.B.A. consultant, attending my first office meeting at Bain & Company, a Boston-based management consulting firm specializing in corporate strategy. The day was organized like an academic conference, with different "case teams" presenting work on various projects they had been doing for clients. It was an opportunity to share intellectual know-how and to familiarize Bain consultants with the kinds of problems we were tackling for clients.

I decided to sit in on the presentation of the Chrysler consulting team because I was curious to find out why Japanese automakers were trouncing U.S. automakers in the marketplace. The "trouncing" I recall was not simply my perception, it was fact: From 1965 to 1985, the combined Japanese market share of worldwide passenger car production jumped from 3.6 percent to 25.5 percent. In striking contrast, the market share of U.S. firms had dropped from 48.6 percent to 19.2 percent.[1]

The Chrysler consulting team manager began the presentation by explaining that they were doing a relative cost position analysis, comparing the cost of a Chrysler car with a comparable Toyota model. The initial analysis suggested that the outlook for Chrysler was dismal. The team found that the total cost of components for the Japanese model was more than 30 percent below that of the comparable Chrysler model. Furthermore, the differences were not confined just to component costs—they extended to quality and speed of new model cycle time. Toyota was receiving customer satisfaction scores 50 percent higher than Chrysler and could develop a new model in 35 percent less time. These were staggering differences in virtually every key measure of performance.

I was intrigued, though not surprised, by the findings and was anxious to see the team's recommendations. However, I was disappointed to find that the Bain team did not have any magical answers for Chrysler that day. Analyzing one component, electrical wire harnesses, the team found that Chrysler was using 21 different suppliers, while Toyota used only two. Thus, one of the key Bain recommendations was for Chrysler to consolidate suppliers. Although this was a reasonable recommendation, it was not particularly satisfying. I did not have any real confidence that Chrysler could make up all of the cost, speed, and quality differences by simply using fewer suppliers. After all, General Motors was "sole sourcing" a large percentage of its components from a small number of large scale in-house suppliers— yet GM was also at a significant cost and quality disadvantage relative to Toyota. Clearly something was going on that we did not quite understand. This day marked the beginning of an intellectual journey bent on discovering the details behind Toyota's, and later Chrysler's, success.

eval of potential
> assess strategic value

bases for colleb.
~ share knowledge
— approp econ of scope from
        distributor / aggregators
— reduce inventory cost + time
        from aggreg.
— demand connection
        > reduces forecast demands + errors
        > reduced cycle time
— dedicated shared assets
— establish interorg. processes
        > discover
        > design
        > implem
        > govern
                > share —

Acknowledgments

———

I owe a tremendous debt of gratitude to those individuals at Chrysler and Toyota who assisted me with my research and who provided me unique access to the inner workings of these extraordinary companies. I would like to thank Chrysler executives Bernie Bedard, Michael Ciccone, John Maples, Dan McDavid, Jesse Nasser, Barry Price, Ed Sprock, Thomas Stallkamp, Jeff Trimmer, and Steve Zimmer for generously giving their time to assist me. I would especially like to thank Bret Hardy for managing the data-gathering process at Chrysler. At Toyota I would like to thank Lesa Nichols, Chris Nielsen, and Hajime Ohba, who provided valuable assistance during my research of Toyota's supplier relations in the United States. In Japan, Junzo Matsumoto, Koichiro Noguchi, Nobuhiko Suzuki, and Michio Tanaka were extraordinarily helpful to me (along with countless other individuals who allowed me to interview them). I would also like to give a special thanks to Matsuo Iwata (formerly of Nissan), who assisted me at Nissan and helped me with the translations of my early surveys.

I also owe a debt of gratitude to the funding agencies that have supported my research through the years. The most important funding program has been the International Motor Vehicle Program (IMVP) at Massachusetts Institute of Technology, where directors Frank Field, Charlie Fine, and Dan Roos have supported my research.

I have also benefited from the research and conversations I have had with other IMVP researchers, notably Taka Fujimoto, Sue Helper, John Paul MacDuffie, Toshi Nishiguchi, and Mari Sako. I would also like to thank the Reginald Jones Center at the Wharton School, University of Pennsylvania, and the National Association of Purchasing Management for funding parts of my research. Without the generous funding of these programs I would never have been able to make the numerous trips to Japan and Detroit that were required to gather the data for this book.

I need to give a special thanks to co-authors and fellow researchers Kentaro Nobeoka, who assisted with my research in Japan, and Wujin Chu and Dong Sung Cho, who assisted me with research in Korea. Not only are they excellent scholars, but they have been good friends and great collaborators. I would also like to thank my research assistants at Wharton, especially John Brookfield, Ben Powell, and Masue Suzuki. I also need to thank, and acknowledge, the intellectual debt I owe to Bill Ouchi, who was my advisor as a Ph.D. student at UCLA and who played an important role in helping me get access to Toyota and Nissan.

Finally, I would like to acknowledge my mother, Bonnie Dyer, and late father, Bill Dyer, for their valuable contributions. I thank my mother for teaching me how to work and for instilling in me a sense of self-confidence. I thank my father for being my intellectual guide and mentor, and for teaching me how to think and reason. Most of all, I want to thank my wife, Ronalee, and my sons, Aaron and Matthew. Ronalee made a direct contribution by helping me with my data gathering and input. She also taught me how to be organized and was very patient during the long trips away to Japan and Detroit. But most importantly, she put up with my long work hours and incessant droning on about Toyota and Chrysler while taking great care of Aaron and Matthew.

Collaborative Advantage

asset composition
matters / built in walls

implications — need forecasts

408 > [theory of form
comparative odds]

what is wrong with to?

Introduction

Collaborative Advantage
and the Extended Enterprise

*Virtual integration means you basically stitch together a business with part-
ners that are treated as if they're inside the company.*

—Michael Dell, C.E.O. Dell Computer

The New Realities of Competition
and Competitive Advantage

This book is about competitive advantage—and more specifically
about how firms create competitive advantages through effective
interfirm collaboration. During the past two decades we have witnessed the rise of "strategic management" as a distinct field of study,
the goal of which is to help firms achieve sustainable competitive
advantage. With the emergence of the strategy field has come a
plethora of new approaches for achieving a competitive edge, each
offering new ideas for improving profits and performance. However,
at a fundamental level, during the past 20 years only two perspectives
have emerged in the field of strategic management regarding the
sources of superior firm performance. The first, or *industry structure
view,* associated with Michael Porter's *Competitive Strategy,*[1] argues
that superior profits are primarily a function of a firm's membership
in an industry with favorable structural characteristics. Porter con-
tends that some industries are inherently more attractive than other
industries due to factors such as few competitors, relative bargaining

power over suppliers and buyers, few substitutes, and barriers to entry. Accordingly, managers are encouraged to enter attractive industries or shape their industries in such a way as to create favorable structural characteristics. Naturally, the search for advantage by both managers and academics has focused on the industry as the relevant unit of analysis.

The second perspective, often described as the *resource-based view*, argues that differential firm performance is fundamentally due to firm heterogeneity rather than industry structure.[2] Firms that are able to accumulate resources and capabilities that are valuable and difficult to imitate will achieve a competitive advantage over competing firms.[3] For example, firms may develop a time-to-market capability, an innovation capability, or an ability to manufacture products at low cost.[4] Thus, the resource-based view focuses on the individual firm as the primary unit of analysis. As long as your individual firm has developed some core competencies (e.g., is efficient, fast to market, innovative, and so forth), then you will achieve a competitive advantage in the marketplace.

Although these two perspectives have contributed greatly to our understanding of how companies achieve superior profit returns, they ignore the important fact that the advantages or disadvantages of an individual firm are often linked to those of the network of relationships in which the firm is embedded. For example, the resource-based view's focus on the single firm implicitly presumes that sources of advantage exist *within the firm*. However, in advanced modern economies, individual firms typically engage in a narrow range of activities that are embedded in a complex chain of input-output relations with other firms. In many cases, firms rely on suppliers to provide highly customized inputs that make up a large fraction of the value of the final product. Indeed, the typical manufacturing firm in the United States purchases 55 percent of the value of each product it produces (this figure is 69 percent in Japan).[5] Moreover, this percentage has been increasing during the past two decades as firms outsource, downsize, and focus on their core competencies.[6] These data highlight the increasing importance of effectively managing and coordinating activities across firm boundaries.

Recent studies suggest that extraordinary productivity gains in the production network, or *value chain,* are possible when companies are willing to collaborate in unique ways, often achieving competitive advantages by sharing resources, knowledge, and assets.[7] In contrast, managers that view the firm, or the industry, as the fundamental unit of analysis for strategy are limited in their perspective and may adopt the wrong strategies for their firms. Today, competition occurs between value chains and not simply between companies.[8] This reality is reflected in both the so-called new economy and old economy. In *Blown to Bits,* BCG consultants Philip Evans and Thomas S. Wurster state, in discussing the new economy, "When all of the functions in a chain are bundled together, what matters is competitive advantage over the entire chain. As long as the sum is advantaged, it does not matter where specifically that advantage comes from, still less whether the business is advantaged in each constituent activity."[9] Consequently, managers need to form a strategy for their entire production network, not just for their company. Indeed, in some industries the production network is the most important unit of competition—firms are achieving competitive success *only* when they assemble a network of firms that know how to collaborate effectively to create unique, valuable, and difficult-to-imitate products and services. In this book I will demonstrate the power of collaborative advantage by showing that Toyota during the 1980s and 1990s and Chrysler during the 1990s have been the highest performing automakers largely because they have organized and managed their production networks more effectively than competitors. Moreover, the principles they have used to create collaborative advantage are applicable to companies in industries ranging from aircraft to computers to software.

I first became keenly aware of the importance of cooperative strategy after seeing a detailed benchmarking analysis that compared the cost and quality of a Chrysler car with a comparable Toyota model. The analysis, which was conducted in 1985, indicated that the total cost of components (70 percent of which were provided by suppliers) for the Toyota model was more than 30 percent below that of the comparable Chrysler model. Furthermore, the differences were not confined to component costs—they extended to quality and speed of new model cycle time. Toyota was receiving customer satisfaction scores 50 percent higher than Chrysler and could develop a new model in 35 percent less time. These were staggering differences on virtually every key measure of performance. These differences undoubtedly explained the dramatic increase in the combined market share of Toyota and other Japanese automakers from 3.6 percent in 1965 to 25.5 percent in 1985. In striking contrast, the market share of U.S. firms dropped from 48.6 percent to 19.2 percent.[10] Moreover, from 1982 to 1998, Toyota was far more profitable than Nissan, its key Japanese competitor, as well as General Motors, Ford, and Chrysler (see Figure Intro.1). These data suggested that Toyota was doing something dramatically different than its competitors. Through years of research, I discovered that the lessons from Toyota are critical for old and new economy companies alike. As David Brooks, director of international product strategy at Microsoft, observed, "The lessons that can be learned from Toyota are applicable beyond the automotive business. They are extremely relevant and important for our business as well."[11]

Seven years later I had the opportunity to study firsthand Chrysler's

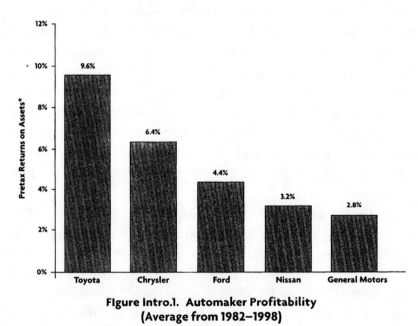

**Figure Intro.1. Automaker Profitability
(Average from 1982–1998)**

(*Source:* Annual reports, Daiwa Analysts Guide)

* Pretax automotive income divided by automotive assets.

attempts to replicate Toyota's methods of organizing and managing its production network. For over five years I was given unique access to people and data at Chrysler, during which time I tracked and documented the events that led to an extraordinary transformation—a transformation that resulted in Chrysler becoming the most profitable and highest performing U.S. automaker in the 1990s.

This book represents eight years of study in the automotive industry—with the explicit goal of providing satisfying answers to the following questions:

- How do we account for Toyota's superior performance relative to competitors in the 1980s and 1990s?
- How do we explain Chrysler's comeback and superior performance relative to Ford and General Motors during the 1990s?
- What are the lessons from Toyota and Chrysler that might be transferable to other organizations?

This book answers these questions and offers rich data on the sources of interorganizational competitive advantage from interviews with over 200 automotive executives and extensive surveys of over 500 suppliers in the United States, Japan, and Korea.

During the past 20 years, numerous theories have been offered to explain the competitive advantage of Toyota and other Japanese firms in complex-product industries, such as automobiles, heavy machinery, robotics, machine tools, and consumer electronics.[12] Without question, Japan's business success in these sectors is remarkable given that it has emerged from the ruins of World War II to achieve the world's second-largest economy and a gross domestic product (GDP) per person that was roughly 20 percent greater than that of the United States in 1996. Informed readers may argue that we already have a sufficient explanation for Toyota's performance advantages: the descriptions of "lean production," or the "Toyota Production System," as described in the 1990 landmark book *The Machine That Changed the World*. Lean production is a new production system that yielded substantial performance advantages for Japanese automakers. However, while the insights from lean production partially explain the creation of high-performance production networks in the auto industry, there is much more to the story than what is told in *The Machine That Changed the World* and other books on automotive success.

This book goes beyond lean production by describing how Toyota and Chrysler have created collaborative advantages by each fashioning a lean *extended enterprise*. By *extended enterprise* I am referring to the set of firms within a value chain or production network that collaborate to produce a finished product (a vehicle in the case of the auto industry). A firm selling to an end market is essentially the culmination of a production network or value chain. For example, Toyota manages a production network that produces the inputs to an automobile. Some of these inputs are produced internally, but most are produced by external suppliers. Thus, the performance of a firm (Toyota) is a function of the performance of a production network (Toyota and its supplier network). When this entire network is lean then the vehicle it produces is most likely to win in the marketplace. Further, when the key players in this production network have created a set of collaboration processes that create conditions of high trust, shared knowledge, and dedicated asset investments that help to create an identity for the production network, then it is an extended enterprise. To achieve stunning performance advantages, it is no longer sufficient to simply create a firm that effectively implements lean production techniques in its own assembly plants.

To illustrate, most studies, including *The Machine That Changed the World*, have highlighted Ford as the U.S. automaker that has most effectively implemented lean production techniques in its own assembly plants. By comparison, Chrysler has been a relative laggard. And yet Chrysler's financial performance has been far superior to Ford's from 1992 to 1998 (see Figure Intro.2). In fact, Chrysler's profit per vehicle and pretax profits as a percent of assets have been *twice as high* as Ford's during that time period. How do we account for this fact? Similarly, Toyota continues to outperform Nissan, and most of its Japanese competitors, despite studies indicating that lean production techniques have diffused widely throughout Japanese industry.[13] If so, why does Toyota continue to have the highest productivity and quality?

Of course, no single theory provides a simple and comprehensive answer to these questions. There are undoubtedly a number of impor-

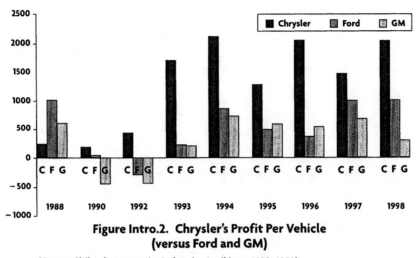

**Figure Intro.2. Chrysler's Profit Per Vehicle
(versus Ford and GM)**

(*Source:* Chilton's *Automotive Industries,* April issue 1988–1998)

tant factors that explain performance differences among automakers. But in the pages that follow, I will describe and document the competitive advantages associated with designing a lean extended enterprise, or a production network that collaborates effectively to achieve *virtual integration.* In the automobile industry, firms primarily compete on time to market, cost, quality, and styling. When a firm is able to establish a lean extended enterprise, it can create advantages in the first three areas; only styling is not directly affected. However, the fact that a lean extended enterprise can deliver a new style to the market more quickly means that the style will be fresher and will be more likely to achieve market acceptance. Thus, I will demonstrate that Toyota and Chrysler's success is based largely on their ability to create the most effective and productive extended enterprises in the industry.

Toyota was the first automaker to recognize that the fundamental unit of competition had changed—from the individual firm to the extended enterprise. In effect, Toyota recognized that not only did it compete with General Motors, but more importantly, the Toyota Group or team of companies, including suppliers, was in competition with both General Motors and its suppliers (see Figure Intro.3). Furthermore, since suppliers produced roughly 70 percent of the value of each Toyota vehicle, Toyota realized that it needed to have the most capable and productive supplier network in the world. They truly

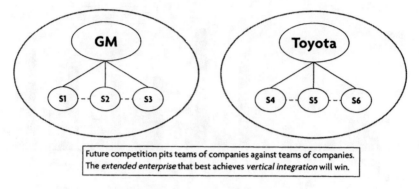

Future competition pits teams of companies against teams of companies.
The *extended enterprise* that best achieves *vertical integration* will win.

Figure Intro.3. Future Competition: Network versus Network

*S = supplier

understood, and took to heart, the old maxim that a chain is only as
strong as its weakest link. Consequently, Toyota developed a set of
interorganizational processes and practices that were designed to create a supplier network that was highly productive, constantly improving, and tightly integrated with Toyota as well as with other Toyota
suppliers. In short, Toyota initiated a level of involvement with, and
understanding of, its suppliers' internal operations that was unprecedented in the industry. As Koichiro Noguchi, a Toyota director who
formerly headed up Toyota's purchasing organization, has observed:
"Our suppliers are critical to our success. We must help them to be the
best.... Quality cars require quality suppliers."[14]

Similarly, Chrysler began to recognize the value of a lean extended
enterprise as it emerged from the brink of failure in the early 1990s. As
previously mentioned, most studies (including the 1999 Harbour
Report) have found Ford to be a leader at implementing lean production techniques in its assembly plants. According to James Womack,
Daniel Jones, and Daniel Roos in *The Machine That Changed the
World,* "Ford has taken lean production to heart" and "is the best example" among U.S. automakers.[15] However, Ford has *not* been the most
effective U.S. automaker at creating a lean extended enterprise.
Chrysler has quietly emerged as the leader in this regard. Chrysler's
extended enterprise has allowed the company to develop new models
more quickly than Ford, and at significantly lower costs. Like Toyota,
Chrysler finally realized that the fundamental unit of competition was

no longer the individual firm but rather the extended enterprise. This new reality is clearly reflected in the words of Thomas Stallkamp, head of DaimlerChrysler's U.S. car operations and Chrysler's head of purchasing during the turnaround, who argues that in today's competitive arena, "the leanest value chain wins."[16] Chrysler's success has prompted Womack and Jones to admit that they "were spectacularly wrong" about Chrysler.[17]

The primary objective of this book is to explain why firm networks are the new unit of competition in the network economy. To accomplish this, I provide a detailed examination of the key characteristics of the lean extended enterprises that have been developed by Toyota and Chrysler. In particular, I examine how these automakers and their suppliers collaborate for competitive success and why some teams of firms (extended enterprises) seem to be able to out-compete others. Thus, this book goes beyond examining the competitive advantages of the individual firm by exploring the sources of interorganizational competitive advantage that can be created within the extended enterprise.

Some readers may wonder whether collaborative advantage is still possible today, given that GM, Ford, and DaimlerChrysler recently agreed to join forces to create a single automotive parts exchange run through the Internet. The idea is to pool their purchasing clout to procure supplies, raw materials, and parts through online auctions. Does this mean that in the future GM, Ford, DaimlerChrysler, and perhaps even Toyota, will purchase standardized parts at the same price, thereby eliminating the possibility of creating collaborative advantage through suppliers? The answer is no and here's why. Although online bidding for low-tech and commodity-like items will increase dramatically, there will still be many customized components for which online bidding will not work. States Tadaaki Jagawa, Toyota's vice president in charge of procurement,

> We meet face-to-face with every one of our suppliers. We are continually traipsing all over the world to see the factories and the managers that make our products, to see if they really make high quality goods. You just can't do that on the Web.[18]

Mr. Jagawa did say, however, that Toyota was likely to participate in the exchange on a limited basis, for example in the trade of "bolts, nuts, and basic office supplies." The point is that the exchange only works for commodity-like products that are *not* customized to a particular vehicle. As long as the vehicle does not become a system of completely standardized modules (something I discuss in the conclusion), collaborative advantage is possible. The action taken by GM, Ford, and DaimlerChrysler is exactly the type of strategy I proposed in an article entitled "Strategic Supplier Segmentation: The Next Best Practice in Supply Chain Management," published in 1998 in *California Management Review* (the key points from the article are elaborated in Chapter 7). In that article I argued that firms should identify those "strategic" suppliers that offer the potential for collaborative advantage and manage them differently from arms-length suppliers (for which I advocated electronic bidding). There are classes of inputs, supplies, and raw materials that are quite standardized and for which online auctions (pure markets) are ideal. States Jeff Trimmer, Daimler-Chrysler's head of procurement strategy,

> We joined the trading exchange with GM and Ford to primarily purchase nonstrategic supplies like office supplies, mops, and rock salt for the parking lots. However, we are absolutely not planning to bid our strategic components jointly with GM and Ford. Mercedes would go ballistic if they had to use the exact same engine components as Ford and GM. Anyone who thinks we will jointly buy all of the same parts as GM or Ford clearly doesn't understand our business.[19]

Mr. Trimmer's message is that there are still engine, transmission, air conditioning, body, and electronic parts that are customized to each vehicle and differentiate it in the marketplace. It is with these suppliers that collaborative advantage is critical.

Organization of the Book and Key Findings

To effectively address the issues regarding how to create a lean extended enterprise, I have organized the book into two sections. The first, comprising chapters 1–4, develops a framework for creating collaborative advantage through the extended enterprise concept. In particular, I focus on four elements of the extended enterprise that are key to its success, as demonstrated by Toyota. Section 2, comprising chapters 5–7, shifts the attention to the United States and examines how Chrysler and Toyota have transplanted Japanese-style supplier relations and the extended enterprise concept to the competitive soil of the United States. In particular, I examine the process that Chrysler went through in creating its own lean extended enterprise. I also examine how Chrysler adapted and modified the *keiretsu* model to work in the United States. (*Keiretsu* is a Japanese word used to refer to a group of Japanese companies that collaborate in partnership fashion.) Similarly, I explore how Toyota has begun the process of creating an effective extended enterprise in the United States.

Chapter 1 introduces the concept of collaborative advantage by arguing that the extended enterprise represents a new unit of competition and competitive advantage. Three key trends are identified as the driving forces behind the extended enterprise as an increasingly important unit of competition. The chapter also outlines a framework for creating collaborative advantage and identifies the four key elements of a lean extended enterprise: designing the boundaries of the firm (or the "governance profile" of the production network, including the make/buy decision); investing in dedicated or relationship-specific assets; creating interorganizational knowledge-sharing routines; and creating high levels of trust throughout the extended enterprise to lower transaction costs and maximize flexibility and responsiveness. In this chapter I argue that a critical core competency for firms today is the ability to design the supply chain, knowing what to do in-house, what to outsource to supplier partners, and what to outsource to arm's-length suppliers.

Simply speaking, Toyota's success is based largely on the fact that its managers know what the boundaries of their firm should be, and they know how to manage their supplier networks effectively. In particular, they avoid vertical integration (except where it is critical for differentiating its vehicles in the marketplace) and they rarely use arm's-length relationships when working with external firms. Furthermore, they have created an identity for their production network so that suppliers feel like they are part of a larger collective (i.e., the Toyota Group). Consequently, individual suppliers in the production network behave as though they were members of the same company. This, in turn, has created the conditions that encourage their suppliers to make investments in assets that are dedicated or tailored to the production network, share valuable knowledge with other members of the production network, and trust Toyota and other members of the production network. The investments in dedicated assets result in a network that is better coordinated than other networks, thereby resulting in lower costs, faster product development cycles, and higher quality. The knowledge-sharing activities result in a production network that learns faster than other production networks about the best practices in production, quality, and management. High trust within the extended enterprise results in a production network with the lowest transaction costs. Less time and effort is spent bargaining and haggling over the pie and more time and resources are spent increasing the size of the pie. Thus, Toyota's tightly integrated extended enterprise—characterized by a high level of dedicated investments, a high degree of knowledge sharing, and a high degree of trust—outperforms the loosely integrated production networks of its competitors.

Chapter 2 describes how investments in dedicated assets (those devoted to the exchange relationship) are critical for value creation within the extended enterprise. By now, most managers know that a key to the success of Japanese network relationships is the practice of dedicating supplier assets to the customer. That is, Japanese automotive suppliers send engineers to work at the customer's site, locate plants near the customer, or invest in customized physical assets. Nevertheless, many U.S. managers do not fully appreciate just how profitable the practice of using dedicated assets can be. In this chapter I describe the types of investments in dedicated assets that create value within Toyota's extended enterprise. I also provide hard data that reveal a distinct correlation between investments in dedicated assets and lower costs, higher quality, and greater profits.

Chapter 3 describes how an extended enterprise continuously learns and develops new capabilities by creating enterprise-wide knowledge-sharing processes, or learning routines. In particular, Toyota's extended enterprise has been superior at transferring valuable knowledge (e.g., on methods to improve productivity, reduce inventories, improve quality, etc.) throughout the entire production network.[20] Not only is Toyota effective at transferring its knowledge to suppliers, but it has created processes that facilitate knowledge sharing among suppliers. Toyota's suppliers actually collaborate with and help each other. In fact, I found that Toyota obtains higher quality parts at lower costs even when it uses the identical suppliers as its competitors. This is possible because Toyota helps the supplier learn and implement best practices within its manufacturing cells devoted to Toyota. Consequently, suppliers use 10 percent fewer workers, have 25 percent lower inventories, and have 35 percent fewer defects in their manufacturing cells for Toyota compared to their other customers. Toyota's extended enterprise simply out-learns competing enterprises.

Chapter 4 focuses on the critical role of trust and effective governance within the extended enterprise. In particular, I describe why trust is critical for reducing transaction costs and maximizing the flexibility and responsiveness of the extended enterprise. I also provide evidence that transaction costs are much higher than most executives think they are—representing as much as 30 to 40 percent of the costs in our economy. I provide some of the first empirical evidence to date which demonstrates that high levels of trust within the extended enterprise can substantially reduce transaction costs. Indeed, Toyota spends only 20 percent of its face-to-face contact time with suppliers negotiating contracts and assigning blame for problems that arise in the course of working together. By comparison, General Motors spends almost 50 percent of its face-to-face contact time with suppliers negotiating contracts and haggling over problems. This partially explains why GM employs almost 10 times the number of people in procurement as Toyota.

Beyond demonstrating that trust creates economic value, I also examine the issue of how to develop trusting relationships within the extended enterprise. Surprisingly, I find that Toyota's ability to develop trust with suppliers is not based primarily on personal relationships between Toyota and its suppliers. Nor is it based primarily on the stock ownership it holds in its *keiretsu* suppliers. Rather, this trust is linked to the perceived fairness and predictability of Toyota's routines for managing external relationships.

Chapter 5 shifts the focus away from Toyota and toward Chrysler in addressing the question: Can U.S. firms create collaborative advantage in the same way as Toyota? In other words, are *keiretsu*-style relationships transferable to the United States? I examine in detail the process used by Chrysler to create a lean extended enterprise in the United States. In particular, I describe how Chrysler transformed its adversarial arm's-length supplier relationships into supplier partnerships. I also examine what Chrysler has done differently than Toyota and what practices they have adapted to fit the U.S. institutional environment. This chapter offers a blueprint for those firms thinking of making a similar transformation.

While chapter 5 focuses on how and what Chrysler changed, chapter 6 describes in detail why these particular changes have produced positive results for Chrysler. In particular, I provide hard evidence that the changes Chrysler has made have dramatically improved the company's performance in the areas of time to market, cost, quality, and profitability.

Chapter 7 outlines the key implementation lessons from both Chrysler's and Toyota's experiences (especially Toyota's experience in the United States) for other firms interested in creating a lean extended enterprise. How does one transform a value chain whose members are loosely connected and internally focused into one whose members are tightly integrated and coordinating effectively as a team? First, I examine the criteria that firms should use in identifying and selecting suppliers for participation in the extended enterprise. Given the high level of resources required to generate value through partnerships, a firm desiring to establish an extended enterprise needs to focus its energies on developing partnerships with those companies that bring high-value, customized inputs to the enterprise. Second, I suggest that successful implementation requires that the orchestrator of the enterprise (e.g., final assembler) know how to create an identity for the enterprise so that member firms feel a mutual co-destiny with other firms in the network. This is vital if the extended enterprise is going to coordinate effectively and behave like a single firm. Third, I suggest that collaborative advantage does not materialize overnight and the orchestrator of the enterprise must patiently put in place and nurture value-creation processes. It takes time for the enterprise to evolve into a value-creation engine for the participating companies.

Finally, the conclusion offers some thoughts regarding the future direction of the extended enterprise and discusses the implications for managers. (I also speculate on the future challenges facing Daimler-Chrysler with regard to pushing ahead with the extended enterprise concept.) For example, in the last few years the idea of the "virtual corporation" has gained considerable attention in the popular press as the wave of the future.[21] Yet, Chrysler's leaders will tell you that if anything their success is based on becoming *less* virtual (in the sense that the players are rapidly changing). Instead, they are developing a stable network of players within their extended enterprise that allows them to achieve *virtual integration*. The final chapter concludes by summarizing why the extended enterprise concept is the key to collaborative advantage. In short, it is the wave of the future.

Application of the Principles Offered in the Book

The insights developed in this book come mostly from the automobile industry, a bellwether that has been dubbed the "industry of industries" by Peter Drucker.[22] Executives in other industries might logically ask: Are these findings generalizable to my industry? Will these ideas work for my company? I believe the answer to that question is an emphatic *yes*, and let me explain why.

In the winter of 1997, after publishing an article about Chrysler's attempts to create an extended enterprise, I received an email from David Brooks, director of international product strategy at Microsoft. Mr. Brooks asked if he could call me to discuss my ideas on collaborative advantage in greater detail. My initial response to his query was: "If there is any company that is powerful enough to go it alone, it's Microsoft. I'm not sure they need to develop collaborative advantages with outside firms." But Mr. Brooks quickly convinced me that Microsoft could benefit greatly from the lessons offered by Chrysler and Toyota. Mr. Brooks explained that Microsoft relies on localization vendors around the world to translate and localize its products in markets as diverse as China, Chile, and Czechoslovakia. Microsoft's time to market and the quality of its products in these markets increasingly depend on the capabilities of its localization vendors. According to Brooks, "Our success in international markets increasingly depends on the skills and capabilities of our localization vendors. Microsoft has often been frustrated with the ability of its suppliers to deliver up to its standards." He went on to explain that he felt that Microsoft could enhance its performance if it could figure out the optimal way to include these vendors in the product development process and if Microsoft could build these supplier's capabilities. Like Microsoft, virtually every company could enhance its competitive position if it could enhance the capabilities of its suppliers or "complementors" and if it could enhance its own ability to learn (issues I address in chapter 3). Thus, I have come to the conclusion that if even mighty Microsoft can benefit from these ideas, then a typical firm which is far less self-sufficient can certainly benefit from these ideas.

This is not to suggest that the ideas presented here are necessarily equally valuable to all firms. In fact, I would expect the ideas to have greater relevance for executives whose business is a *complex-product* industry like automobile manufacturing. The findings reported here are most applicable to other similar complex-product industries. I define a *complex product* as a knowledge-intensive product "comprising a large number of interdependent components, functions, and process steps."[23] Complex-product industries tend to be characterized by a high degree of reciprocal interdependence on the part of firms in the value chain.[24] When tasks are not routine and interdependence and uncertainty is high, information processing shifts from impersonal rules to personal, and idiosyncratic, exchanges. Investments in dedicated assets and interorganizational knowledge-sharing routines are often necessary to coordinate on non-routine tasks that are reciprocally interdependent. Examples of industries that fit these characteristics include bulldozers, trucks, aircraft, heavy machinery, robotics, machine tools, computers, software, microelectronics, telecommunications, biotechnology, consumer electronics, and so forth. However,

I have witnessed the trends that I describe in this book—which are changing the way firms should organize their value chains—affect industries that would not necessarily be described as complex-product industries, such as textiles, oil and gas, and utilities. Moreover, the ideas found in chapters 2–4 regarding how to create value through dedicated asset investments, effective knowledge management, and trust in firm networks are very relevant to "horizontal" firm networks (multipartner ventures) such as Iridium (where companies from different industries like Motorola, Raytheon, Lockheed Martin, and others collaborate in an alliance to attack a new business opportunity).

Guiding Principles of the Extended Enterprise

This book addresses the following questions and offers the following guiding principles for managers and executives of firms in complex-product industries.

- *What are the appropriate boundaries of the firm? To what extent should I vertically integrate versus source from the outside using arm's-length relationships or partnerships?* The guiding principle with regard to the boundaries of the firm, or what I call the governance profile of the firm, is to vertically integrate only when integration is critical for product differentiation and use arm's-length market relationships less than has been done historically. Most U.S. manufacturers would benefit by transforming arm's-length relationships to partnerships and spinning off in-house component divisions.
- *What strategy (or strategies) should I employ in managing outside suppliers? When should I use partnerships versus arm's-length relationships?* The guiding principle with regard to arm's-length relationships versus partnerships is to use arm's-length relationships when inputs are low value; commodities or standardized (open architecture) products; stand-alone, or modular with no or few interaction effects with other inputs; and characterized by a low degree of supplier-buyer interdependence. In contrast, partnerships are preferable with outside suppliers that produce inputs that are high value; non-standard

inputs or (closed architecture) inputs with the potential to differentiate the final product; and characterized by a high degree of supplier interdependence and which have multiple interaction effects with other inputs.

•   *What are the processes involved in collaborating effectively with outside firms (notably suppliers) in order to achieve a competitive advantage? How exactly do supplier partnerships create competitive advantage?* The competitive advantages that are possible through effective partnerships are based on greater investments in dedicated or relationship-specific assets in the production network, more effective knowledge sharing within the production network, and higher trust and lower transaction costs within the production network. These are mutually reinforcing factors that can substantially increase the effectiveness and speed with which the production network can solve complex problems.

In summary, this book is particularly relevant for managers and executives who want to know more about creating and managing successful supplier networks. As the boundaries of firms continue to blur, executives must become more skilled at coordinating the efforts of teams of companies. This book examines how some companies are creating competitive advantages through more effective interfirm collaboration.

The DaimlerChrysler Merger

This book was researched and written before the merger of Chrysler and Daimler-Benz. Currently, the combined firm is still seeking to optimize the strengths that each company brought to the marriage. At the time of the merger, some people questioned why Daimler-Benz, a successful luxury car company with tremendous brand equity, high quality, and a loyal following at the profitable high end of the car market, would want to merge with Chrysler, a firm with mid- to low-end vehicles, lower quality, and less brand equity. Of course, the advantages for Chrysler seemed obvious: Joining with Daimler-Benz would enhance the cachet of its brands, and Daimler's engineering prowess might help Chrysler improve the quality and performance of its vehicles. But did Daimler-Benz actually expect to learn anything of value from Chrysler? In fact, it is clear that one of the reasons that Daimler-Benz was eager to merge with Chrysler was to learn from Chrysler's clear lead in the United States in time to market with new models and lowest cost per vehicle structure. As noted in a *Fortune* article, "Chrysler can give the Germans some lessons about efficiency and speed to market."[25] At the time of the merger, Chrysler was developing a new vehicle almost 25 percent faster than was Daimler-Benz. Furthermore, Chrysler was generating the highest profit per vehicle in the United States on vehicles sold mainly at the middle to lower end of the market (Daimler-Benz was focused almost completely on luxury cars and had no experience making, or making money, on mid- to low-end vehicles). Chrysler's strengths were due primarily to the competitive advantage of its extended enterprise. As noted in *The Economist*, "it [Chrysler] survives thanks only to its distinctive and lean way of involving suppliers in its innermost thinking."[26] Daimler-Benz recognized that Chrysler was doing something quite different from its U.S. competitors and that Chrysler might offer valuable lessons for its organization. The fact that a third-generation Chrysler executive, Gary Valade, has been put in charge of worldwide purchasing for the new DaimlerChrysler is a promising sign. But the integration of Daimler and Chrysler operations will not be without its challenges. Chrysler is a lean North American producer which buys 70 percent of its value-added components from outside; Daimler is a more fully integrated German maker of luxury cars, famed for its world-class design.[27] Chrysler is known as having a decision-making and managerial philosophy that pushes from the bottom up; Daimler from the top down.[28] The concern about how Chrysler will be integrated into Daimler is reflected in an article in the *Economist:* "Daimler will be tempted to impose its methods on Chrysler. But it has more to learn than it realizes from Chrysler's manufacturing skills. If it fails to recognize this, it is in for real trouble."[29] Unfortunately, the trouble may have started. Thomas Stalkamp, Chrysler's procurement head during its turnaround and DaimlerChrysler chief of U.S. operations resigned (some say was forced out) a year after the merger due largely to philosophical differences with Daimler chief Juergen Schrempp. Daimler-Chrysler's stock dropped 5.6 percent, which translated into a drop in market vale of $4 billion. Clearly Stallkamp's expertise in building and managing Chrysler's extended enterprise was highly valued by the market. Whether or not Daimler, and other companies, can learn and benefit from Chrysler's experience is yet to be seen.

1

Creating Partnerships
for Collaborative Advantage

> The battlefront in today's competitive wars, and the ultimate core compe-
> tency of a business organization, is the design of the supply chain.
>
> —Charles H. Fine, *Clockspeed*

The Driving Forces Behind Network Competition

In the introduction, I argued that the extended enterprise is an important new unit of competition and that successful firms must be able to create partnerships with other firms in the production network. But why are production networks and interfirm partnerships so important today? Or perhaps the better question is: Why is interfirm collaboration more important today than it was in the past? Recent data show that in just the past two years there have been more than 20,000 new alliances reported worldwide.[1] What is driving the rapid growth in alliances? Has something fundamentally changed to make alliances a necessary part of a firm's strategy, as well as a more effective way to compete? To answer these questions it is necessary to examine the different options firms have for organizing their value chains and some key trends that have influenced the relative efficiency of different value chain organizations. In this chapter I will describe why the design of the supply chain is critical to a firm's competitive success. I will also show why most firms should increase their use of partnerships with suppliers while decreasing their use of vertical integration and arm's-length supplier relationships.

Alternative Ways of Organizing
the Production Network

When organizing a firm or production network an executive must resolve two issues: the degree of vertical integration (what to make versus buy) and the supplier management strategy.

During the past 20 years a branch of economics, called *transaction-cost economics,* has produced a useful theoretical framework for guiding a firm's decisions with regard to sourcing the various components or subsystems of a product or service. According to transaction-cost theory, there are three basic alternatives for governing (or sourcing) a transaction (supply chain) relationship:

- *vertical integration or hierarchy,* meaning the firm produces the required input in-house and maintains control over both the sourcing unit and the buying unit; at the extreme, a firm would provide all its own inputs.
- *arm's-length relationships or markets,* meaning the firm buys inputs from outside using a number of short-term suppliers and shops for the best price each time it requires an input.
- *partnerships or alliance,* meaning the firm buys from a small number of suppliers and builds long-term, cooperative relationships with those few suppliers.

According to transaction cost theory, when inputs are highly customized and involve transaction-specific or dedicated assets, firms should vertically integrate. (There are a number of terms that have been used to describe assets that are customized to an exchange relationship, including *transaction-specific assets, relationship-specific assets,* and *dedicated assets.* I will generally use the latter term in connection with these types of non-redeployable investments.) Vertical integration is preferred when inputs must be highly customized because the buyer reduces the transaction costs associated with bargaining over the profits generated in a customized exchange. In contrast, when inputs are highly standardized, or do not involve transaction-specific assets, firms should use arm's-length relationships with outside suppliers who can specialize and achieve economies of scale. Finally, partnerships fall in between vertical integration and arm's-length relationships. Partnerships are preferable when economies of scale are important but when the transactors can create value through some investments in dedicated assets.

When deciding which of these options to chose, managers must wrestle with a fundamental dilemma: Productivity grows with the division of labor, thereby creating an incentive to outsource activities to more specialized firms, but specialization increases the costs of communication and coordination of activities, thereby creating an incentive to bring activities in-house to manage under a common hierarchical structure.

During the past 75 years, the dominant organizational strategy of U.S. automakers, and most other firms in the United States, has been to vertically integrate those activities that required close coordination and that the firm wanted to control, and buy on the market all other inputs from outside suppliers. Items purchased from the outside tended to be those for which there were specialized suppliers with economies of scale. Buying firms typically used competitive bidding as a way to acquire uniform inputs from markets at the lowest possible price. Thus, the production network of most manufacturing firms was organized as a set of vertically integrated activities combined with the inputs of a group of arm's-length suppliers. General Motors has been a prime example of a firm that is highly vertically integrated (GM has produced internally roughly 65–70 percent of the components that go into a vehicle) but which also sources externally primarily through arm's-length relationships.

During the past decade many firms, including GM, have found that historical decisions concerning the desired level of vertical integration are badly outdated, with serious effects on competitiveness. For example, shortly before he stepped down as chairman at General Motors, Roger Smith noted that GM's vertical integration, the most extensive in the industry, "had ceased to be a 'strategic advantage' and had become a 'semi-disadvantage.' " What Smith described as a semi-disadvantage was in fact "a per-car cost disadvantage sufficient to produce staggering losses, while leading to a nearly crippling loss of market share."[2] In fact, for some time now we have witnessed less vertically

integrated firms in the computer and auto industries, Dell and
Chrysler for example, "stealing customers from rigid, vertically integrated rivals like IBM and General Motors."[3] States Dell CEO, Michael
Dell, "If you look back to the emergence of any industry—and this is
certainly true of the information industry—you will find that most
companies integrated vertically to gain scale and provide maximum
value to customers." Dell goes on to argue that virtual integration is
replacing vertical integration. "The shift from vertical to virtual integration ... makes it possible to bring customers and suppliers inside
your business; to share openly critical business information; to create
true information partnerships."[4]

Not only has vertical integration seemingly become a liability, but
the arm's-length model of supplier management is also under fire.
Indeed, arm's-length relationships are becoming increasingly obsolete
in complex-product industries. The primary liability of the arm's-
length model is that suppliers will not make the dedicated investments
or share the knowledge necessary to coordinate effectively to produce
a differentiated, complex product. However, there are at least three
additional reasons that the arm's-length model has fallen out of favor.
First, the administrative or transaction costs associated with managing a large number of vendors often outweigh the benefits. In some
cases, the administrative and inventory holding costs associated with
arm's-length bidding practices can actually outweigh the costs of the
parts themselves. In my study I found that GM uses roughly 10 times
the number of people as Toyota to manage its large supply base. Second, dividing purchases across multiple suppliers reduces the ability
of suppliers to achieve significant economies of scale.[5] Moreover, buyer
bargaining power may increase as much, or perhaps more, by increasing purchases from a single supplier. As Chrysler purchasing chief
Thomas Stallkamp observed, "We have found that the more we buy
from a particular supplier, the more responsive the supplier is to our
needs."[6] Finally, firms have discovered that vigorous competition can
be achieved with just two suppliers as long as the suppliers are equally
competent and managed skillfully.[7] Toyota maintains effective competition between just two suppliers by adjusting volume between the
suppliers based on their performance.

In place of arm's-length relationships and vertical integration, new organizational forms have been emerging that rely increasingly on partnerships, or relationships that are neither arm's-length in character nor governed by hierarchy. These have been referred to variously as *alliances, partnerships,* or *value-added partnerships.* When a group or network of firms collaborate in partnership fashion, this is sometimes referred to as a *strategic network, virtual corporation,* or *extended enterprise* (the latter is the term I will use consistently throughout this book). These forms involve new and different types of relationships between firms. But these organizational forms have not emerged in a vacuum. Three key trends have placed vertical integration and arm's-length relationships at a disadvantage relative to partnerships as a way to organize the value chain (see Figure 1.1).

Current Trends That Favor Network Partnerships

Trend #1: Advancements in Information Technology

Historically, effective coordination of complex tasks typically had to occur within a firm. Why? Because within firm boundaries it was possible to co-locate individuals who needed to coordinate, and it was also possible to make investments in firm-specific communication technologies and routines. Firms have always been better than markets at coordinating on complex tasks. However, recent advances in computing and telecommunications have dramatically reduced the costs and increased the speed and quality of communications across firm boundaries. These technologies have become so powerful and

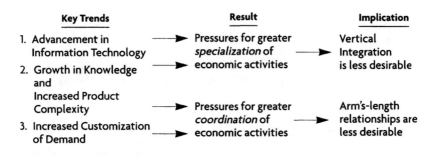

Key Trends	Result	Implication
1. Advancement in Information Technology	Pressures for greater *specialization* of economic activities	Vertical Integration is less desirable
2. Growth in Knowledge and Increased Product Complexity		
3. Increased Customization of Demand	Pressures for greater *coordination* of economic activities	Arm's-length relationships are less desirable

Figure 1.1. Trends That Disfavor In-House and Arm's-Length Sourcing

inexpensive that they allow legally distinct firms to collaborate effectively on increasingly complex tasks. Consider the fact that in 1980 the
primary means for communicating across firm boundaries was either
by telephone or mail. Today, firms have overnight mail, fax machines,
e-mail, the Internet, and video conferencing as vehicles for interfirm
communication. To illustrate the extent to which communication costs
have decreased, in 1983 (the first year that fax machines could talk to
each other using a common standard) the price (in constant 1998 dollars) of the average fax machine was roughly $1,495.[8] Today the aver-
age cost of a fax machine is less than $200. Thus, costs have dropped
by approximately 90 percent. Similarly, the cost of a three-minute telephone call between New York and London has fallen from approximately $43 (in 1998 dollars) in 1970 to $1 today.[9] E-mail offers the
ability to send files and documents around the world within minutes
at virtually no cost.

The ease with which firms can communicate across firm boundaries has further increased due to the emergence of standard-setting
bodies for communication machines. For example, before 1983 fax
machines made by different companies could not talk to each other,
and it was impossible to fax a document to another firm unless they
had purchased their fax machine from the same vendor. This is not a
problem today. A variety of technologies based on common standards
permit the instantaneous sharing of information between organizations. In many cases, these technologies allow for coordination of
highly complex tasks. For example, compatible computer-aided-design
software and electronic-date interchange have improved the ability of
organizations to coordinate effectively in product design functions,
thereby allowing separate firms to coordinate on the complex tasks of
product design and development.

Trend #2: Increasing Knowledge and Product Complexity

The body of potentially commercializable knowledge is growing at
an accelerating pace. To illustrate, Joseph Badaracco Jr. points to the
growth in scientific journals as evidence of an explosion in the development and specialization of knowledge: "There were roughly 100

scientific journals in 1800, about 1,000 by mid-century, and roughly 10,000 in 1900 ... according to the World List of Scientific Periodicals ... we are now well on the way to the next milestone of 100,000 such journals."[10] In a similar vein, a study by strategy consultant McKinsey & Company found that the percentage of "knowledge workers" in the United States has increased dramatically over the past few decades. (Examples of knowledge workers include senior managers, supervisors, engineers, scientists, technicians, and so forth.) The study found that in 1930 only 30 percent of U.S. workers were knowledge workers, whereas by 1994 that had more than doubled to 62 percent.[11] Due to this growth in knowledge and knowledge workers, the research and development investments required by individual firms to stay at the cutting edge of a knowledge frontier have increased. Consequently, firms are increasingly focusing their resources on a narrow set of specialized activities, or core competencies.

The growth in knowledge has also resulted in increasingly complex products. Consider, for example, how the complexity of an automobile has changed over time. A colleague of mine described how, during the 1920s and 1930s, his uncles disassembled and reassembled their Ford Model T cars on the weekends as a hobby. This was possible because the knowledge embedded within the assembly of the automobile was relatively accessible, requiring only simple tools and a basic knowledge of assembly and mechanical engineering. Back in the 1950s, any kid with ambition, a modicum of talent, and a set of socket wrenches could do impressive things under the hood of a car. One did not need thousands of dollars in diagnostic equipment and a degree in computer science to work on a 1955 Ford. Today, however, those same individuals would not even be able to make relatively basic repairs on a Ford vehicle without considerable training and a sizable investment in the proper equipment. The knowledge embedded in automobile assembly has grown exponentially and has been accompanied by a dramatic increase in the use of computers and electronics. Staying on the cutting edge of automotive assembly and repair requires a focused effort of resources and attention on a narrow set of activities. To extrapolate, staying at the cutting edge of technologies that influence the effectiveness of automotive braking systems, air conditioners, seats, or a variety of other automobile subsystems or components requires a focused effort of resources. These are all activities performed internally, and less efficiently, by General Motors, whereas Toyota and Chrysler use supplier partners who are focused on those activities as their core competencies.

The accelerating pace of knowledge growth suggests that production networks should be less and less integrated within single firms, and more and more characterized by highly focused and specialized firms that can make the research and development investments necessary to stay at the frontier of a knowledge domain. Thus, the growth in knowledge should result in *less* vertical integration, with more specialized firms having the advantage. However, while the growth in knowledge has pushed production networks toward more specialized and focused firms, the increased interdependence of components and subsystems required to make complex products has driven the demands for effective coordination across functions and firms, with the result that arm's-length relationships are increasingly disadvantaged relative to partnerships.

Trend #3: Increased Customization of Demand

Another reason that the demands for effective coordination across firm boundaries have increased is due to a rise in customization of demand. During the past two decades we have witnessed the emergence of increasingly differentiated products designed for increasingly demanding and sophisticated customers. No longer is it sufficient to develop standardized, mass-produced products for a large middle-class market, where customers are willing to accept the same product. Customers want, and can afford, products that meet their particular needs. The result is *mass customization*—the phenomenon of trying to mass produce tailored products.[12] However, to be truly effective at customizing individual products for given customer segments, it is often necessary to involve the supply chain to a greater degree than ever before. Simply buying standardized inputs from suppliers will not result in the differentiated products demanded by the marketplace. As a result, partnerships are a superior way to work with suppliers that are asked to make customized inputs.

Of course, it is possible for a firm to design a unique product and then set up a bidding contest to select a supplier to provide unique inputs. But this often results in a product that is both costly to produce and does not effectively meet customer needs. Why? First, it is extremely costly for suppliers to make unique products for a customer, particularly when the suppliers cannot contribute to the design in a way that takes into account their current manufacturing capabilities. Second, when the supplier is not involved in the product-development process, it is not able to contribute its relevant knowledge to the design to ensure that the product will truly meet the customers' needs. Consequently, to most effectively meet differentiated customer needs, the product-development process demands relationships with outside firms that are characterized by a greater degree of interdependence and coordination than ever before.

Implications for Organizing a High-Performance Extended Enterprise

These trends outlined above have placed vertical integration and arm's-length relationships at a disadvantage relative to partnerships as a way to organize the value chain because there are greater needs for specialization and coordination than ever before. So how does a production network achieve both a high degree of specialization and a high degree of coordination? It can be done through the effective use of partnerships within the extended enterprise. While arm's-length relationships allow for a high degree of specialization, they are a poor way of achieving a high level of coordination across firms. Likewise, while vertical integration allows for effective coordination across functions and tasks, it is a poor way to achieve the level of focus and specialization required to stay at the cutting edge of a knowledge domain. The problem is that production networks need both a high level of specialization and a high level of coordination to occur *simultaneously*. Thus, partnerships are an increasingly superior way of sourcing inputs relative to markets and hierarchies. Using partnerships within the extended enterprise concept both solves the problem of specialization, allowing firms within the production network to specialize as necessary, and solves the problem of coordination by creating rules, norms, and procedures (just as firms do) for coordinating and sharing the knowledge required to produce complex and customized products. In many ways, the production network must behave like a single firm. When the group of firms view each other as partners and collaborate effectively for the good of the larger group, then they have established an extended enterprise characterized by virtual integration.

As a practical matter, getting firms to specialize is much less difficult than getting firms to effectively collaborate because the forces driving specialization—notably economies of scale and the explosion of knowledge—push firms increasingly to specialize. The real challenge is figuring out how to get a collection of relatively autonomous, self-interested firms, who often have a bargaining relationship with their neighbors in the value chain, to collaborate and coordinate in the development of complex, customized products. This is a particularly difficult task because individual firms within a production network have incentives to maximize their own profits, and this often comes at the expense of a firm adjacent in the value chain (i.e., a supplier or customer). Thus, firms do not naturally trust each other, share information, or engage in other activities that result in productivity improvements for the production network as a whole.

A Comparison of Governance Profiles in the Automobile Industry

Let us take a moment to apply these ideas to the automobile industry. If accurate, this analysis would suggest that, over time, we should see an increased use of partnerships in the automotive industry and a coinciding decrease in vertical integration and arm's-length relationships. It would also predict that a production network characterized by a high degree of vertical integration and arm's-length relationships would be at a disadvantage relative to a production network that effectively uses partnerships.

An examination of differences in the use of vertical integration, arm's-length relationships, and partnerships reveals that Toyota is much more likely to use a heavy mix of partnerships, whereas competitors General Motors and Ford are more likely to use a heavy mix of vertical integration and arm's-length relationships. Figure 1.2 depicts the percent of total vehicle component costs that are internally manufactured (vertically integrated), the percent purchased from partner suppliers, and the percent purchased from arm's-length suppliers. We can call this a firm's *governance profile*. A governance profile refers to the percent of inputs (by value) that are governed internally (by hierarchy), by arm's-length relationships (which rely primarily on legal contracts), and by partnerships (external relationships governed by trust and implicit long-term agreements rather than legal contracts). Doing an "apples to apples" governance profile comparison between Toyota and GM/Ford is possible for internally manufactured products, but much more difficult to do for arm's-length relationships and partnerships. In this particular analysis, the automaker is believed to have an arm's-length relationship with suppliers when they use three or more suppliers to provide parts in a particular part category (e.g., batteries, radiators, air conditioners, spark plugs, and so forth). This fits the definition of rotating purchases to a number of suppliers on a short-term basis. However, partnerships are much more likely to exist when the automaker uses only one or two suppliers in a given product

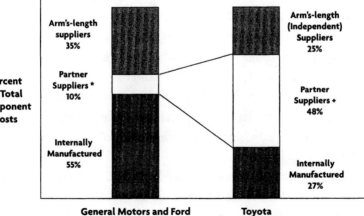

· Two or fewer suppliers for a product category
+ *Kankei kaisha*

**Figure 1.2. Governance Profile
(Toyota vs. GM and Ford)**

category and relies on long-term relationships with those suppliers. Toyota only internally manufactures about 27 percent of its components, whereas General Motors and Ford internally produce double that figure, or roughly 55 percent. Toyota is much less vertically integrated and, therefore, its production network is populated by many more specialized firms. Furthermore, when Toyota does source from the outside, it is much less likely to use numerous suppliers, or arm's-length relationships, (only 25 percent) and much more likely to use partnerships (48 percent). In contrast, when Ford and General Motors purchase from the outside, they are much more likely to use arm's-length relationships (35 percent) instead of partnerships.

How does this compare to Chrysler's governance profile? In 1989, when Chrysler first began its transformation, its governance profile looked a lot like General Motors' and Ford's, although Chrysler was less vertically integrated. During the last few years Chrysler has reduced its degree of vertical integration by spinning off a number of in-house parts divisions to its partner suppliers, including its plastics division to Textron, its electric wiring division to Yazaki, and its seat-covering operations to Johnson Controls Inc. Overall, since 1985 Chrysler has decreased its level of vertical integration from roughly 50 percent to 30 percent.[13] At the same time, Chrysler has reduced its supply base by more than 60 percent and has transformed its relationships with suppliers from adversarial to cooperative and trusting (we will examine how Chrysler accomplished this in chapter 5). Thus, today Chrysler's governance profile looks very much like Toyota's, with roughly 30 percent of parts manufactured internally and less than 25 percent produced by arm's-length suppliers or by suppliers in component categories where Chrysler rotates purchases among three or more suppliers. Chrysler relies primarily on partnerships with suppliers as the way to source its inputs.

The governance profiles employed by Toyota and Chrysler during the 1990s were systematically different than the governance profiles employed by General Motors and Ford. Toyota's and Chrysler's production networks were characterized by both greater specialization (due to less vertical integration) and greater coordination (due to fewer arm's-length relationships). This is a key factor contributing to the superior profit performance of Toyota and Chrysler. Ford and General Motors have finally become aware of the liabilities of their governance profiles and have each made efforts to change. Ford has spun off a number of its internal parts divisions (as Visteon) and has recently attempted, with mixed success, to develop Japanese-style partnerships with its arm's-length suppliers.[14] Likewise, General Motors has moved to consolidate and spin off a number of in-house parts divisions in its Delphi Automotive unit.

I should point out that the optimal governance profile may differ somewhat from industry to industry. For example, although complex-product industries demand high levels of coordination, and thus a higher percentage of vertical integration or partnerships, simple product industries are likely to demand a higher percentage of arm's-length relationships. To illustrate, the success of Japanese firms has been primarily in complex-product industries, such as autos, heavy machinery, robotics, machine tools, and consumer electronics. The Japanese share of world production of these products is substantially higher than Japan's share of world gross national product would suggest it should be.[15] Conversely, for products or services with comparatively less complex production processes, such as paper, food processing, petrochemicals, retailing, and bulk pharmaceuticals, Japanese firms are considerably less efficient than their U.S. competitors.[16] Why might this be the case? The answer has much to do with the governance profiles of Japanese firms. Japanese automakers, and Japanese companies in general, are less vertically integrated and rely more on partnerships than their U.S. counterparts. On average, Japanese automakers are roughly 50 percent less vertically integrated than U.S. automakers, and the Japanese manufacturing industry in general is 30 percent less integrated than U.S. industry.[17] Thus, they have a much more specialized and decentralized economy, as evidenced by the fact that two-thirds of the Japanese labor force are in establishments of under 300 workers, while in the U.S. two-thirds are in establishments of over 300 workers.[18] However, while Japanese firms outsource the majority of their inputs, they rarely have true arm's-length relationships with outside suppliers. The prevalence of alliances in Japan has prompted some scholars to refer to Japan as an "alliance economy" that relies on "alliance capitalism."[19] In fact, the ability of Japanese firms to create effective interfirm partnerships is key to their ability to coordinate in the development and production of complex products. However, in mature industries with simple production technologies and processes which utilize standard inputs, the Japanese propensity to use alliances places them at a disadvantage because: (1) investments in relationships and coordination mechanisms are costly and are not justifiable given a lesser need for interfirm coordination, and (2) firms are unable to easily switch suppliers for standardized inputs even when it may be economically rational to do so. For example, in a study of Japanese purchasing managers, Professor Mari Sako found that Japanese purchasing managers occasionally "lamented not being able to make a clean, though drastic, break with unwanted sub-contractors."[20] In many cases Japanese firms should use arm's-length relationships but for cultural reasons they do not. Thus, the Japanese propensity to use alliances is likely to have its liabilities in industries characterized by less complexity where coordination is less important.

Even within an industry, the optimal governance profile may vary somewhat from firm to firm, depending on each firm's individual strategy. For example, Volvo has attempted to differentiate its vehicles based upon safety features, appealing to those buyers who are most safety conscious. As a result, it would make more sense for Volvo to vertically integrate into safety-related subsystems and components, or to at least develop partnerships with outside firms to develop cutting-edge, state-of-the-art safety features with those suppliers. However, these are differences at the margin. Volvo cannot stray too far from a governance profile that relies heavily on partnerships (similar to Toyota and Chrysler's) or else, over time, it will likely find itself increasingly at a disadvantage.

Gaining Advantage Through Partnerships

Of course, performance improvements do not come automatically just because a firm outsources more and uses fewer suppliers that they call partners. Partnerships only create value when they are managed effectively and as they take on characteristics that are different from arm's-length relationships. By examining the relevant characteristics of arm's-length market relationships, we find clues that guide our search for *collaborative advantage,* or competitive advantage that is generated through effective partnerships.

Arm's-length market relationships are characterized by a lack of dedicated asset investments; minimal information exchange (i.e., prices act as coordinating devices by signaling all relevant information to buyers and sellers); separable technological and functional systems within each firm that are characterized by low levels of interdependence (e.g., the two organizations typically have only a sales-to-purchasing interface); and low need for trust because neither party is vulnerable and switching costs are low. As a result, most of these relationships are governed by simple legal contracts.[21] Under these conditions it is easy for buying firms to switch suppliers with little penalty because other sellers offer virtually identical products. Efficiency in the execution of routine tasks is the strength of market relationships. Thus, arm's-length market relationships are incapable of generating collaborative advantage because there is nothing idiosyncratic about the exchange relationship that enables the two parties to generate profits above and beyond what other seller-buyer combinations can generate. The relationships are not rare or difficult to imitate.

Partnerships generate competitive advantages *only* as they move the relationship away from the attributes of market relationships. In other words, the competitive advantages of partnerships are linked to three major factors (see Figure 1.3). The first factor, *dedicated assets,* refers to investments in factories, equipment, processes, and people that are customized to a particular customer or supplier. These investments improve the productivity of the network and the speed with which the network can coordinate in developing unique products. The second factor, *knowledge-sharing* routines, refers to systematic and purposeful attempts on the part of suppliers and customers to exchange valuable, and oft times proprietary, knowledge. This could be knowledge about the market, production processes, quality, delivery, design, safety, or anything else that may help each firm to learn how to be more efficient and effective. The final, and perhaps most important factor, is *trust.* The degree of trust between firms, or trustworthiness of a

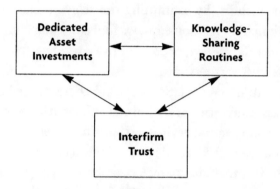

**Figure 1.3. Three Key Sources of Interorganizational
Competitive Advantage**

partner, can be measured as the partner's history of following through
on promises and commitments, and a partner's refusal to take advantage even when it has the chance. Trust is critical for partner success
because without it suppliers and customers will spend considerable
resources negotiating, monitoring, and enforcing inflexible contracts.
In short, the transaction costs in these exchange relationships will be
extremely high. In addition, without trust the exchange partners will
be unwilling to make investments in dedicated assets (because these
types of investments are not easily redeployable and the firm making
the investments is at risk) and to share useful knowledge (because they
will not trust how the knowledge will be used). Thus, trust facilitates
both investments in dedicated assets and knowledge sharing. Similarly, it is typically the case that investments in dedicated assets improve
coordination, thereby resulting in greater knowledge sharing between
firms. Likewise, greater knowledge sharing results in the alliance partners' discovering new ways to create value in the exchange relationship
through dedicated investments. Thus, dedicated asset investments and
knowledge sharing are also mutually reinforcing factors.

Conclusion

This chapter examined why business partnerships are mushrooming
in unprecedented fashion. I identified advancements in information
technology, growth in knowledge and product complexity, and

increased customization of demand as three key trends that are making interfirm partnerships more attractive as an organizational form compared to vertical integration and arm's-length relationships. These trends are creating pressures for both greater specialization and greater coordination of work activities. Partnerships have the potential to provide both. I introduced the idea that each company has a governance profile—or a mix of vertical integration, partnerships, and arm's-length relationships—as the methods for governing transaction relationships, or sourcing of inputs for a final assembled product. I also argued that the optimal governance profile in a complex-product industry like the automobile industry is characterized by a heavy mix of partnerships relative to vertical integration and arm's-length relationships. I showed that the highest performing automakers, Toyota and Chrysler, have governance profiles that rely heavily on partnerships, whereas Ford and GM have had governance profiles that rely heavily on vertical integration and arm's-length relationships. Finally, I argued that partnerships do not automatically create value, but must be managed effectively in order to generate high levels of investment in dedicated assets, knowledge exchange, and trust. In the next three chapters I will describe exactly how Toyota has achieved collaborative advantage by building an extended enterprise based on trust, investments in dedicated assets, and shared knowledge.

2

Creating Dedicated Assets
in the Extended Enterprise

Our objective is to locate our plants as close to Toyota as possible. It's necessary for us to be physically close in order to make eight just-in-time deliveries per day and to communicate effectively.

—Vice president of sales, Toyota supplier

We're surrounded by parts vendors. We can scream for it, "Bring parts!"

—Minolta plant manager

By now, many U.S. managers know that the formidable success of Toyota and other Japanese manufacturers stems to a great extent from their close relationship with suppliers. Toyota and others, working closely with their respective lean-production networks of parts suppliers, produce high-quality products quickly and inexpensively. And competitors rooted in traditional mass-production operations, which have typically compelled manufacturers to keep suppliers at arm's length, are left struggling to catch up. Why? As suggested in the previous chapter, arm's-length relationships are less able to provide the coordination required for the effective development and manufacture of complex products. Partnerships are a more effective way of providing high-level coordination, primarily because the supplier and buyer are more willing to invest in relationship-specific or dedicated assets. A key to Toyota's success is the practice of dedicating supplier assets to the customer. That is, Toyota's suppliers send engineers to work at the customer's site, locate plants near the customer, or invest in customized physical assets. As a result, Toyota is able to keep transportation and inventory costs low and improve product-development coordination.

Nevertheless, many U.S. managers still do not fully appreciate just how profitable the practice of using dedicated assets can be. They incorrectly assume that new information technologies (described in the previous chapter) are a perfect substitute for physical proximity and face-to-face contact. Although it is true that new communication technologies make physical location and face-to-face contact less important today, they are still critical when developing a complex product. And all else being equal, coordination between firms is enhanced through physical proximity and face-to-face contact. My study of production networks in the auto industry strongly reinforces the contention that assets dedicated to the production network provide Toyota with substantial competitive advantages. In particular, my research on Toyota and Nissan and 96 of their first-tier suppliers, and on Chrysler, Ford, and General Motors and 125 of their direct suppliers, reveals a distinct correlation between the practice of using dedicated assets and lower costs, higher quality, and greater profits.

Dedicated Assets

Dedicated assets are investments made by one firm in the value chain that are specialized to those of other firms in the chain. Firms can invest in three different types of dedicated assets in order to increase productivity in the production network: site specialization, physical asset specialization, and human specialization. *Site specialization* refers to the location of successive production stages in close proximity to one another to improve coordination and economize on inventory and transportation expenses. For example, a supplier may locate its factory next door to a major customer factory in order to minimize transportation costs and inventories while supplying just-in-time. *Physical asset specialization* refers to relationship-specific capital investments (e.g., in customized machinery, tools, information systems, delivery processes, and so forth) that allow for faster throughput and greater product customization. Physical asset specialization allows for

tion of the institutional environments and cultures within the two countries. However, if we compare Toyota's production network with Nissan's we find that the differences are smaller but still significant. (I compared Toyota with Nissan because up until the mid 1990s, Nissan was roughly four times larger than any of Toyota's Japanese competitors, including Honda; Honda has only recently emerged as a strong competitor to Toyota in Japan.) Nissan's plant configuration is not nearly as concentrated as Toyota's (see Figure 2.4). Nissan's assembly plants are spread primarily around the Tokyo area with plants typically between 20 to 50 miles apart. Nissan's affiliated and independent supplier plants are located farther away than Toyota's suppliers, with the average plant distance being 53 and 172 miles, respectively. As a result, Nissan suppliers make half as many daily deliveries as Toyota's suppliers. Not surprisingly, Nissan also has significantly less face-to-face contact with suppliers compared to Toyota.

The close geographic proximity of Toyota's extended enterprise is a key reason why it is more productive than GM or Nissan. Beyond the

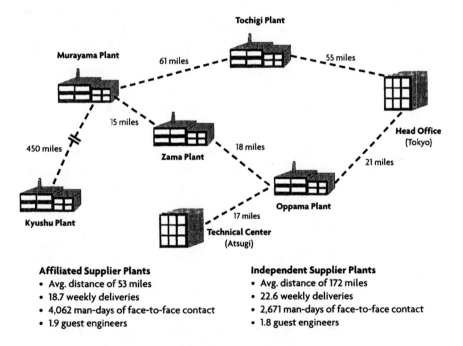

Affiliated Supplier Plants
- Avg. distance of 53 miles
- 18.7 weekly deliveries
- 4,062 man-days of face-to-face contact
- 1.9 guest engineers

Independent Supplier Plants
- Avg. distance of 172 miles
- 22.6 weekly deliveries
- 2,671 man-days of face-to-face contact
- 1.8 guest engineers

Figure 2.4. Nissan Plant Configuration in Japan

(*Source:* Dyer 1996)

advantages of lowering inventories and transportation costs, a geo-graphically concentrated production network also facilitates the for-mal and informal dissemination of information and technology across firms in the network. It substantially lowers the costs of face-to-face communication, which is critical when communicating and transfer-ring complex knowledge. This is one reason that Toyota's supplier net-work learns faster than competitor supplier networks (in chapter 3 I will demonstrate that Toyota's supplier network does learn faster).

Well aware of the advantages of geographically proximate plants in its production network, Toyota has replicated this strategy outside Japan. After it set up an assembly plant in Georgetown, Kentucky, in 1986, roughly 90 suppliers followed Toyota to Kentucky. In addition, Toyota has completed building its second assembly plant in the United States. Not surprisingly, it is located literally next door to the first plant. Toyota is not alone in its understanding of the importance of physical proximity. Honda has followed a similar strategy in setting up its pro-duction network in the United States. Honda's Ohio complex consists of two automobile assembly plants, a motorcycle assembly plant, an engine and transmission facility, and a major research and develop-ment facility.[1] More than 65 transplant suppliers have followed Honda and set up operations in Ohio. In fact, in a survey of Japanese trans-plant suppliers, over 90 percent reported that the most important rea-son for selecting a plant location was so that they could be physically close to a particular customer. Proximity to the customer was more important than labor costs, a non-union environment, government assistance, availability of skilled labor, and a host of other factors.[2] Most U.S. companies simply do not appreciate this fact to the same degree.

The Value of Human Specialization

Toyota places an extremely high value on face-to-face communication with their suppliers. For example, although suppliers are located nearby, Toyota insists that they assign engineers, called *guest engineers*, to work full time at Toyota's technical center in Toyota City. When the suppliers' engineers have desks in the same room as the automaker's engineers, it is easy to coordinate activities. Direct interaction is also a more efficient way to communicate complex, dynamic information during the development of new vehicle models.

A Japanese purchasing manager stressed the importance of face-to-face communication with suppliers:

> When we first built a plant in the United States, we began sourcing many parts locally, though the part was often designed by us or one of our suppliers in Japan. We would send the design blueprints to the U.S. suppliers and ask them to produce it. But many of the U.S. suppliers could not build the part according to the drawings because they claimed that too many details had been left out. We had to meet with these suppliers and incur the additional costs of making various details understood and explicit. Unfortunately, one of our U.S. suppliers began producing parts according to the design without checking with us first. The parts were not right, and we refused them. The supplier threatened to sue us, and there was some tension until we finally worked things out. I can't remember having a similar problem with one of our Japanese suppliers.[3]

This purchasing manager went on to point out that direct communication and long-standing relationships with their Japanese suppliers made explicit written communications largely unnecessary. In fact, in their early vehicle launch experiences, Toyota's North American suppliers underperformed dramatically in the entire development process relative to Toyota's Japanese suppliers. These supply-chain blunders delayed by as many as 10 months the launch of the Camry and Avalon vehicles and raised development costs.[4] Indeed, for some critical parts Toyota took the unprecedented step of arranging for backup or "shadow" suppliers in Japan, whose overnight air-freight costs were as high as $1 million a month.

Over time, Toyota's relationships with its North American suppliers have become more efficient as human specialization has increased. By working together, individual employees from both Toyota and its North American suppliers have developed specialized knowledge—and a shared language—that allow them to catch errors and communicate more effectively.

The result of Toyota's emphasis on communication is greater efficiency, faster product-development cycles, and more reliable products.
An examination of the relationship between defects per 100 vehicles
and man-days of face-to-face contact between automakers and suppliers clearly supports the relationship between communication and
quality (see Figure 2.5). Toyota engages in an average of 7,235 man-days
of face-to-face contact per year with suppliers and houses more than
700 supplier guest engineers at its technical center—an average of
roughly 4.5 engineers per supplier. Moreover, Toyota's engineers and
managers work at suppliers' sites on either a permanent or a temporary basis. Roughly 20 percent of the top managers (*yakuin*) at Toyota's
affiliated suppliers are former Toyota employees, and these individuals help suppliers coordinate with Toyota. In contrast, Nissan houses 2
guest engineers per supplier at its technical center in Atsugi and aver-
ages 3,344 man days of face-to-face contact with suppliers. Though
lower than Toyota's figures, Nissan's are still considerably higher than
the comparable figures for GM—only 0.2 guest engineers per supplier
and 1,106 man-days of face-to-face contact with outside suppliers.

Toyota's, Nissan's, and GM's varied emphasis on face-to-face communication and reliance on guest engineers correlate directly with
figures on defects per 100 vehicles. According to J.D. Power and Asso-

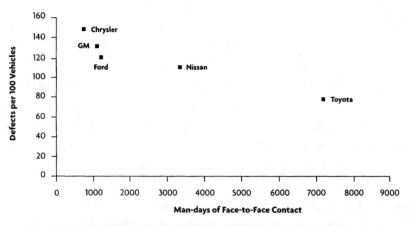

**Figure 2.5. The Relationship Between Face-to-Face Contact
and Vehicle Quality**

ciates, from 1990 to 1995, Toyota's cars had an average of 20 percent fewer defects than Nissan's cars and 40 percent fewer defects than GM's, Ford's, and Chrysler's. These figures should not be surprising since various studies have shown that quality increases when there are fewer suppliers and less variation in people and organizational processes,[5] and when there is an increase in the speed of feedback and reliability of data both within and across firms in the production network.[6] A key way to reduce variation, increase the reliability of feedback, and improve collaboration is to increase human specialization between supplier and customer. In particular, when supplier and buyer engineers develop relation-specific know-how and have substantial experience working together, they are less likely to misread blueprints or misinterpret information.[7] As human specialization increases, the feedback loop becomes more efficient. Fewer communication errors and more effective feedback, in turn, result in higher quality.

Dedicated face-to-face communication also speeds up product-development cycles, which is a critical source of competitive advantage in many industries, including the automotive.[8] Historically, car model sales (in units) have increased more than 20 percent in both the United States and Japan after a major model change.[9] Thus, automakers who are able to develop new models more quickly than competitors have an advantage because their current models are more advanced and include the latest in technology.[10] Since the majority of automotive parts are produced by suppliers, the ability of automakers to coordinate design and manufacturing effectively with suppliers is critical.

Toyota, with its greater emphasis on direct contact with suppliers, has gained the heralded advantages of time-based competition. For example, over the past two decades, Toyota has been able to develop a new car model in just 50 months—almost 40 percent faster than automobile manufacturers in the United States. More recently, Toyota developed a new vehicle model in a record-breaking time of 18 months from concept approval to volume production.[11] Toyota also recently announced that it could deliver a customized order in 5 days, 25 days faster than the industry average of 30 days. These speed advantages are possible largely because Toyota and its suppliers have a long history of working together and have developed coordination routines based on a high level of face-to-face communication and investments in electronic data interchange. As a result, engineers at both suppliers and at Toyota develop knowledge of who knows what, who can help with what problem, or who can exploit new information. It includes awareness of where useful expertise resides within the extended enterprise. In turn, this increases the speed with which Toyota and its suppliers can solve the problems associated with new product development.

In summary, human specialization is critical for success when developing complex, knowledge-intensive products with many production steps, which is where Japanese manufacturers have primarily been successful. Indeed, it is the ability to coordinate human activity that lies at the heart of competitive advantage in complex-product industries.

The Value of Physical Asset Specialization

Toyota suppliers in my study reported that roughly 22 percent of their total capital investments were so dedicated to their primary customer that these customized physical assets could not be redeployed if the customer walked away. In contrast, U.S. suppliers indicated that about 15 percent of their investments could not be redeployed. Previous studies have concluded that Japanese suppliers take more responsibility for the detailed engineering of parts and are more likely than U.S. suppliers to develop unique parts for their customers. For example, as Harvard Business School professor Kim B. Clark and Tokyo University professor Takahiro Fujimoto noted in their book *Product Development Performance*, 38 percent of U.S. automaker parts were off-the-shelf parts, compared with only 18 percent of Japanese parts.[12] In other words, Japanese automakers use a higher percentage of parts that are customized to fit a particular model. Clark and Fujimoto's study suggests that dedicated assets play an important role in the improvement of product integrity and thus in overall product quality. Of course, greater product customization and higher quality may also lead to higher costs. However, Toyota and its suppliers fight these cost penalties with lean-production techniques that minimize changeover times.

Another example of how dedicated assets can improve performance can be found in the different delivery (trucking) practices used by Toyota and its U.S. competitors. U.S. automakers are more likely to use numerous trucking companies (an average of 4.2) that are less likely to arrive on time for pickup and who do not have side loading capability. In contrast, Toyota uses only one trucking company in the United States and this company has made investments in trucks with side loading trailers. Side loading trailers reduce the time spent loading the truck, both at the suppliers' dock and at Toyota. As a result it only takes 35 minutes (on average) for a supplier to load a truck for Toyota whereas it takes 58 minutes to load a truck for GM and Ford.[13] This practice speeds throughput and reduces inventories throughout the production network.

Toyota's production network is characterized by greater site, human, and physical asset specialization than its U.S. or Japanese competitors. This allows the production network to coordinate more effectively and is key to its ability to produce a higher quality vehicle, in shorter development times, and with lower inventory costs. These dedicated investments at least partly explain why Toyota has been twice as profitable as the other automakers during the past 15 years and its affiliated suppliers have been 50 percent more profitable than other Japanese or U.S. suppliers.

Why Not Vertically Integrate?

A natural question one might ask is: If dedicated investments create so much value, can't a firm achieve this same level of dedicated asset investments by simply vertically integrating and forcing the relevant parties to make the investments? The answer is yes. Vertical integration is an option. However, while vertical integration has some coordination advantages relative to partnerships and arm's-length relationships, it does not come without its liabilities. In fact, vertical integration has specific liabilities in complex-product industries operating under conditions of uncertainty. These include loss of high-powered incentives, loss of scale and access to outside customers, loss of strategic flexibility, and higher labor costs.

Loss of High-Powered Market Incentives

The first liability of vertical integration is a loss of high-powered incentives.[14] The standard logic is that while vertical integration may reduce opportunism, it increases "shirking" costs by breaking the strong connection between output and rewards. High-powered incentives are particularly important in industries characterized by a great degree of technological and demand uncertainty (e.g., the auto industry), to encourage executives and managers to put in the extra effort necessary to respond effectively.

U.S. automaker in-house component divisions have few, if any, direct competitors and therefore have less incentive to improve. Moreover, it is difficult for one division to "fire" a sister division for poor performance.[15] Division managers within a U.S. automaker have less incentive to perform since they have less access to the residual profits than do managers at a supplier. U.S. parts division managers typically do not reap large rewards from improved performance. In contrast, suppliers have strong incentives to improve and perform.[16] Managerial efforts to reduce costs or improve the product will result in higher profits and salaries for themselves, a better future for employees, or, in difficult times, survival instead of bankruptcy.

Loss of Scale and Access to Outside Customers

Vertical integration results in a loss of access to outside customers, which is costly for two reasons: a loss of economies of scale in production and a loss of information from external customers, who provide a rich source of ideas.[17] When companies vertically integrate into parts production they often underestimate the impact of competing with customers. Some firms refuse to buy from a particular supplier if they are competing in any other product markets. For example, historically Ford has had an explicit policy of not buying components from GM parts divisions.[18] This partly explains why less than 10 percent of GM's parts divisions' sales have been to outside customers. This can be particularly problematic for the vertically integrated firm because the minimum efficient plant sizes of upstream and downstream activities (in the value chain) are rarely the same.[19] As a result, component manufacturers generally need to sell some output to the market (e.g., to customers who may be direct competitors). Vertically integrated suppliers are often in a no-win situation. If they produce a part that is viewed as advanced or technically superior, they may be prohibited from selling to external customers. For example, to protect proprietary knowledge, in the past GM's internal parts divisions were required to get approval before selling parts to other automakers.[20] However, if the component is not differentiated or superior to other products on the market, then external customers will virtually always refuse to buy from a supplier who is also a competitor. The result of this catch-22 situation is a loss of economies of scale (which is critical in standardized products) and/or limited access to new customers, new technology, and new ideas (which is critical for innovation and differentiation). No matter which strategy is chosen, the vertically integrated supplier is disadvantaged relative to the independent supplier.

Loss of Strategic Flexibility

Another liability of vertical integration is that it may result in a loss of flexibility, which is critical when uncertainty is high. Vertical integration increases the size of an organization, producing additional layers of management and greater centralization. Greater centralization increases the distance of most subordinates from their ultimate superiors, which results in communication distortions and slowed decision making. The inability of GM's internal parts divisions to independently raise capital is an example of the constraints on decision making imposed by hierarchy. Historically, GM's internal supply divisions could not borrow independently, and investment and capital expenditure decisions needed to be authorized at the corporate level. This placed constraints on an internal supplier's ability to respond to market demands. The Automotive Components Group (ACG) at GM (now Delphi Automotive) "felt that it would spend 30–40 percent more if it were an independent company, and that its cash flow could support the additional expenditures. Many of the components divisions felt cash-constrained; for example, Inland Fisher Guide [a GM division] spent less than 1 percent of sales on R&D whereas its competitors spent 3 percent or 4 percent."[21]

Higher Labor Costs

Finally, vertical integration increases the size of the firm. Of course, size alone is not necessarily a problem. However, large firms typically pay higher wages and give more benefits to employees at all levels than do smaller firms.[22] Moreover, as firms get larger, the strength of organized labor increases, thereby allowing workers to appropriate a larger percentage of the profits.[23] The auto industry serves as an excellent example of this phenomenon. United States automakers pay 35 percent higher hourly wage rates than U.S. auto industry suppliers and 88 percent higher wages than suppliers from the general manufacturing base.[24] Similarly, Japanese automaker wages are 32–47 percent higher than suppliers'.[25] Quite simply, automakers that are more vertically integrated will be at a labor cost disadvantage.

To illustrate how vertical integration can place a company at a labor cost disadvantage, let us compare GM with Toyota and Chrysler. To begin, GM produces roughly 35 percent more of its parts internally compared to Toyota or Chrysler. Further, since labor represents roughly 15 percent of the total cost structure, GM is at an overall cost disadvantage on 5 percent of its cost structure (or 0.35 x 0.15). Assuming GM pays 35–40 percent higher wages than suppliers, GM would be at an overall cost disadvantage of roughly 2–3 percent relative to Toyota and Chrysler, owing solely to its higher labor costs in its vertically integrated parts divisions.

In summary, while vertical integration is always an option, due to the liabilities described here firms should be very careful about producing in-house when there are outside suppliers with similar capabilities. This explains why partnerships may be superior to vertical integration as a way to create an extended enterprise with high levels of investment in dedicated assets.

Conclusion

There is a positive relationship between investments in dedicated assets and the performance of a production network. A cursory examination of the features of some high-performing firms in other complex-product industries suggests that this central thesis applies to other situations as well. For example, Trek has emerged as a leader in high-performance bicycles with an astounding 48.4 percent annual growth rate since 1990. Trek rapidly develops state-of-the-art designs faster than competitors at its "all in one" campus in Waterloo, Wisconsin, where all marketing staff, engineers, designers, and manufacturing personnel work within a 10-minute walk of one another. Similarly, Professor Anna Lee Saxenian describes how Hewlett Packard and other Silicon Valley firms have greatly improved performance by developing long-term partnerships with physically proximate suppliers. Saxenian claims that "proximity greatly facilitates the collaboration required for fast-changing and complex technologies which involve ongoing interaction, mutual adjustment, and learning."[26] As Sun Microsystems materials director Scott Metcalf has observed, "In the ideal world, we'd draw a 100 mile radius and have all our suppliers locate plants into that area."[27] Various studies offer similar examples from the semiconductor, disk drive, and business-imaging industries.[28]

In terms of a conceptual framework, I appear to be advocating increased investments in dedicated assets in all situations. However, this approach may not always be appropriate. Undoubtedly there is a point at which additional face-to-face contact merely consumes additional resources. Furthermore, advances in computer-aided machine tools are making it easier to create customized products without investing in dedicated equipment and machinery. The optimal level of specialization between firms in a production network is likely to be contingent on product complexity and the degree of interdependence. Generally speaking, the greater the product complexity and interdependence among components in a final assembly, the more both parties will benefit from investments in specialized assets. My argument here is simply that U.S. managers often do not consciously consider the entire production network when they make important decisions such as where to locate their plants and facilities. Instead, they focus primarily on costs such as the cost of land, labor, taxes, and so forth. I have not yet seen "cost of coordination with supply chain" as a line item in plant location cost models. My work suggests that U.S. automakers have systematically underestimated the importance of human and site specialization. As a result, on some dimensions their extended enterprises cannot achieve the same level of performance when competing against Toyota's tightly integrated and specialized extended enterprise.

3

Effective Knowledge Management in the Extended Enterprise

The ideas behind the Toyota Production System have basically diffused and are understood by our competitors. But the know-how regarding how to implement it in specific factories and contexts has not. Toyota Group companies are better at implementing the ongoing *kaizen* activities associated with the Toyota Production System. I think we are better at learning.

—Michio Tanaka, general manager
of international purchasing, Toyota Motor Corporation

Recently both executives and academics have argued that in today's world of hypercompetition, a firm's ability to learn faster than its competitors may be the *only* sustainable competitive advantage. "Knowledge-management" has become a hot topic as managers seek to help their firms develop a learning capability. But how exactly do firms learn? And why do some firms learn faster than others?

To answer these questions, it is first important to recognize that companies do not learn in a vacuum. Indeed, much of the knowledge that is relevant to a firm's continued success has likely been developed *outside the firm*. Thus, one of the key challenges for companies is to identify and access valuable knowledge that resides in other firms (for example, suppliers, customers, and complementors). Moreover, companies increasingly do not compete alone. As companies outsource more of their value chain to suppliers, their competitive advantage depends increasingly on the performance of those suppliers. This rings true in industries ranging from automotive to software. For example,

Toyota relies on suppliers for more than 70 percent of the value of its vehicles and suppliers play a key role in building quality into Toyota vehicles. As Toyota director, and former purchasing head, Koichiro Noguchi argues, "Our suppliers are critical to our success. We must help them to be the best." In a very different industry, software, even powerful Microsoft relies on "localization vendors" around the world to translate and localize its products in markets as diverse as China, Chile, and Czechoslovakia. Microsoft's speed to market and the quality of its products in these markets increasingly depends on the capabilities of its localization vendors. States Microsoft's director of international product strategy David Brooks, "Our success in international markets increasingly depends on the skills and capabilities of our localization vendors." Like Toyota and Microsoft, many companies could enhance their competitive position if they could enhance the capabilities of their suppliers or "complementors" and if they could enhance their own ability to learn. But most companies are leery of trying to actively improve their suppliers. Not only is it difficult to work across companies, but if a company tries to improve a supplier's performance, it may be helping its competitors who also buy from that supplier.

Toyota, well-known for having the strongest supplier network in the automobile industry, shows a way out of these problems. Over the years it has invested heavily in networks of communication among its suppliers, at first between Toyota and each supplier but eventually among suppliers by themselves. (The big U.S. automakers, by contrast, do not even have supplier associations.) The networks promote the spread of successful practices, involving both explicit and tacit knowledge. By insisting that all relevant knowledge be nonproprietary (with just a few exceptions), and by carefully subsidizing knowledge-sharing activities within the extended enterprise, Toyota has gained the cooperation and energetic participation of its suppliers. And because of the essential inertia of supply chains, surprisingly little of this knowledge has been transferred to production lines for Toyota's rivals.

In this chapter I will demonstrate that firm networks that consciously facilitate knowledge flows among members have tremendous learning advantages. The reason is really quite simple. Knowledge is a resource characterized by what some people call "perfectly increasing returns."[1] This means that if you invest to learn something once and that knowledge can be reused at (almost) zero additional cost, when you double the number of uses the cost per use drops in half. This is extremely relevant to networks of firms because as the nodes (firms) in a network increase arithmetically, the value of the network increases exponentially. In a two-firm network, knowledge can only flow two ways. In a four-firm network, knowledge can flow 12 ways. But in a six-firm network, knowledge can flow 30 ways. Thus, adding a few members can dramatically increase the value for all members. This explains why a small innovation (say in kanban methods) at one firm can ripple (be adopted) throughout the production network at relatively low cost and end up creating tremendous value for the overall network. Toyota is the master at making this happen in its extended enterprise.

In the following sections I will describe how Toyota has created knowledge-sharing supplier networks in both the United States and Japan. In particular, I examine how Toyota achieves two key goals: getting suppliers in the network to actively share knowledge with Toyota and each other; and minimizing the spillover of knowledge to competitors. I also demonstrate that Toyota's extended enterprise wins in part because it is able to "out-learn" the networks of its competitors.

Toyota and Its Suppliers
Learn Faster than Competitors

Interorganizational learning is critical in the automobile industry. Why? Because automobiles are developed and manufactured by automakers (Original Equipment Manufacturers or OEMs) and their supplier networks, who produce as much as 70 percent of the value of a vehicle. Consequently, the cost and quality of a vehicle are a function of the productivity of a network of collaborating firms. Research to date suggests that Toyota's production network has been superior at transferring productivity-enhancing knowledge throughout the network.[2] For example, Professor Marvin Lieberman examined the diffusion of lean production practices as measured by labor productivity improvements and inventory reductions by automakers and their suppliers from 1965 to 1990.[3] Lieberman found that in Japan, labor productivity (as measured by value added per employee) increased steadily and consistently for both automakers and suppliers over 25 years (see Figure 3.1). In contrast, the labor productivity of U.S. automakers and suppliers was stagnant until the mid 1980s, when U.S. automaker productivity began to increase. These labor productivity increases began when Toyota and other Japanese automakers established transplants in the United States (U.S. figures include transplants) and when U.S. automakers were seriously attempting to imitate lean production practices.[4] However, these productivity improvements did not spill over to U.S. suppliers, whose productivity remained stagnant until roughly 1990. Why is this the case?

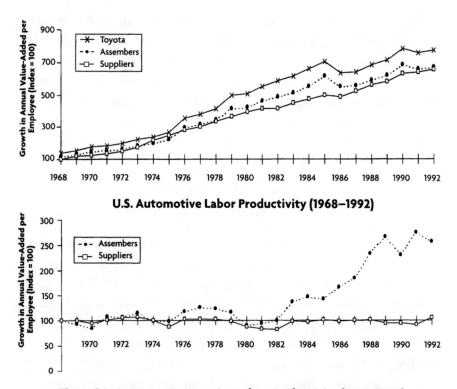

U.S. Automotive Labor Productivity (1968–1992)

Figure 3.1. Japanese Automotive Labor Productivity (1968–1992)

(*Source:* Adapted from M. Lieberman, 1994. "The Diffusion of 'Lean Manufacturing' in the Japanese and U.S. Automotive Industry." "Revolutionary Change" Conference, Sizuoka, Japan.)

The answer is that Toyota and its suppliers have superior knowledge-transfer mechanisms when compared to other automakers and their supplier networks. As a result, they are able to increase worker productivity, lower inventories, and improve quality at a faster rate than competitors. And this is true not only in Japan, but also in the United States. Indeed, my research convincingly demonstrates that Toyota does more to help its U.S. suppliers learn than do the suppliers' Big Three automaker customers. Moreover, my research shows that Toyota's U.S. suppliers learn faster in their operations dedicated to Toyota than they do in their operations dedicated to their Big Three customers. In this chapter I examine the structures and processes that allow for effective interorganizational learning within Toyota's extended enterprise. I also describe how Toyota solves problems inherent in knowledge sharing, such as free-rider problems and preventing undesirable spillovers.

How Toyota Facilitates Learning Within its Extended Enterprise

Toyota has developed an infrastructure, including a wide range of organizational routines, that facilitates the transfer of knowledge within its extended enterprise. Since our focal interest in this chapter is knowledge sharing within a network of firms, it is useful to define what I mean by *knowledge*. Most scholars divide knowledge into two types: *explicit knowledge or information*, and *tacit knowledge or know-how*.[5] Explicit knowledge is easily codifiable and can be transmitted "without loss of integrity once the syntactical rules required for deciphering it are known." Explicit knowledge includes facts, axiomatic propositions, and symbols, such as information on the size and growth of a market, production schedules, and so forth. By comparison, tacit knowledge or know-how involves knowledge that is "sticky," complex, and difficult to codify.[6] It often involves experiential learning. Examples of tacit knowledge include knowledge of how to change a manufacturing cell from a mass-production process to a flexible production (i.e., Toyota production) process, or how to implement new quality techniques such as poke yoke. Because tacit knowledge is the most complex and difficult-to-imitate knowledge, it is likely to generate competitive advantages that are sustainable. Indeed, Ikujiro Nonaka and Hiroyuki Takeuchi make the case in *The Knowledge-Creating Company* that the really powerful form of knowledge is tacit knowledge, because it is the primary source of creative new products and ways of doing business.[7]

Toyota has two major divisions that take the lead in coordinating supplier learning activities: purchasing and Operations Management Consulting Division (OMCD). When necessary, purchasing and OMCD involve other Toyota divisions, such as the Quality Assurance Division (QAD) and Manufacturing Operations Division (MOD), to work together to solve problems with suppliers. Toyota has established six key routines that facilitate knowledge sharing within its extended enterprise (see Table 3.1).

Toyota's Supplier Association

Toyota's supplier association (*kyohokai*) in Japan was established in 1943 to promote "mutual friendship" and the "exchange of technical information" between Toyota and its parts suppliers. In 1996 Toyota's *kyohokai* had three stated purposes: information exchange between member companies and Toyota, mutual development and training among member companies, and socializing events.[8] To achieve these

Table 3.1. How Toyota Facilitates Learning in Its Supplier Network

Process	Nature of the Transfer Process	Type of Knowledge	Toyota Functions Involved
1. Supplier Association	Multilateral	Explicit Knowledge (some tacit knowledge)	Purchasing
2. On-site Consulting	Bilateral	Tacit Knowledge	OMCD/TSSC
3. Supplier Learning Teams (*Jishuken/PDA* Groups)	Multilateral	Tacit Knowledge	OMCD, LAD
4. Problem-Solving Teams	Bilateral	Tacit Knowledge	QAD, MOD OMCD, LAD
5. Employee Transfers	Bilateral	Tacit Knowledge	Purchasing, Personnel
6. Performance Feedback; Process Monitoring	Bilateral	Explicit Knowledge	Purchasing

Note: OMCD=Operations Management Consulting Division; TSSC=Toyota Supplier Support Center; MOD=Manufacturing Operations Division; QAD=Quality Assurance Division; LAD=Logistics Administration Division.

purposes, Toyota's *kyohokai* is divided into three regions: Tokai *kyohokai* (150 members) for the Tokai region (Aichi prefecture, where Toyota City resides); Kanto *kyohokai* (65 members) for the Tokyo region; and Kansai *kyohokai* (29 members). Toyota has created three separate regional associations because it recognizes that for the associations to achieve their objectives, the suppliers must be in close geographic proximity (e.g., within three to four hours by car or train). Toyota also established an equipment supplier association (*eihoukai*) in 1983 that currently has 77 members and is designed to achieve the same purposes as the *kyohokai*.

Toyota started its U.S. supplier association (Bluegrass Automotive Manufacturers Association, or BAMA) in 1989 with only 13 suppliers. Involvement was voluntary and most of the initial members were U.S. suppliers and Japanese transplants located in close proximity to the Georgetown, Kentucky, plant. The initial objective was to provide a regular forum for sharing information with suppliers and for eliciting supplier feedback. Even though few suppliers joined, Toyota pushed ahead, making BAMA meetings as valuable for suppliers as possible. Gradually, word spread through the supply base that these meetings were useful. By 1997 the association had grown to 97 suppliers. Toyota's Chris Nielsen, assistant general manager for purchasing planning, stated:

> We really didn't know if this would work in the United States. Getting suppliers to talk to each other was a key element of the program. Before BAMA, it was not very natural for supplier executives to talk and share information. It was uncomfortable. Over the years that has changed significantly as suppliers have built relationships at senior levels.[9]

The organization of Toyota's supplier association is outlined in Figure 3.2. The general assembly, top management meetings, and executive meetings are designed to allow for high-level communication within the supply network with regard to production plans, policies, market trends, and other issues. Thus, these meetings are designed to share explicit knowledge among members. More frequent interaction occurs within the divisional committees and topic committees (cost,

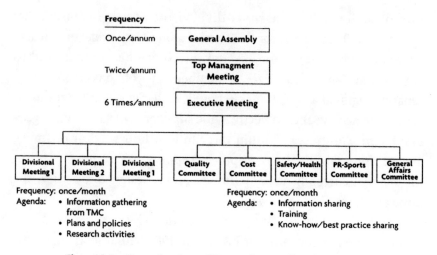

Figure 3.2. Organization of Toyota's Supplier Association

quality, safety, etc.), where members engage in both explicit and tacit knowledge sharing. Divisional committees are comprised of suppliers who join the meetings because of the nature of the parts they produce or the production processes they employ. For example, division committee 2 is comprised of suppliers who primarily supply parts to the powertrain (engine, transmission, etc.) of Toyota vehicles. This allows Toyota and its suppliers to share knowledge about parts that must interface with each other.

The topic committees on cost, quality, safety, and general affairs are designed to facilitate knowledge sharing on subjects that are critical to all members in the extended enterprise. One of the keys to getting suppliers to participate in knowledge sharing activities is to start by sharing knowledge that can clearly benefit every supplier. An examination of one of these, the quality committee, illustrates the important role that the topic committees play.

The quality committee, established in 1961, engages in a number of activities designed to improve the quality capabilities of members of the supply network. The committee picks a theme for the year (e.g., the 1994 theme was "Eliminating supplier design defects") and meets six times each year to share knowledge with regard to that particular theme. These themes are selected by suppliers (with Toyota's input) in areas believed to be important to a large number of members in the network. The quality committee also sponsors three different programs. The basic quality training course enrolls approximately 100 engineers each year. The 5-session, 12-day course takes 96 hours to complete. Excellent plant tours allow suppliers and Toyota to visit "best practice" plants both inside and outside the automotive industry so that members can see firsthand the processes used by firms that achieve high quality. A quality management conference is held once each year and offers Toyota suppliers the opportunity to learn from lectures delivered by experienced Toyota directors and senior managers, as well as from case studies of six successful quality improvement cases. The six supplier cases—two plant managers' cases, two supervisors' cases, and two quality circles' cases—are selected from write-ups submitted to a committee panel by member companies. In 1995, 146 out of 150 Tokai *kyohokai* members submitted cases to the conference.

In summary, the supplier association's primary objective is to develop relationships among suppliers and provide a forum for sharing valuable knowledge. The supplier association is a particularly important vehicle for creating an identity for the Toyota production network or Toyota Group (the importance of this will be discussed in greater detail in chapter 7). Membership in the association makes suppliers feel like they are part of a larger collective.

Consulting Teams

Toyota's Operations Management Consulting Division (OMCD) was established in the mid 1960s by Taiichi Ohno to help solve operational problems both at Toyota and at suppliers. OMCD is the organizational unit within Toyota assigned the responsibility to acquire, store, and diffuse valuable production knowledge that resides within Toyota's extended enterprise. OMCD currently consists of 6 senior and highly experienced executives (each with responsibility for 2 Toyota plants and approximately 10 suppliers) and about 50 consultants. Approximately 15–20 consultants are permanent members of OMCD while the rest are "fast track" younger individuals who are expected to deepen their knowledge of the Toyota Production System (TPS) through a rotation (usually 3 years) at OMCD. These senior executives and consultants are the gurus of TPS. OMCD helps suppliers by sending them a team of consultants for a period of time ranging from one day to many months, depending on the nature of the problem. This assistance is free to suppliers, who are not charged for the consultants' time. This is an extended enterprise resource that is accessible to all members. My survey of 38 first-tier Toyota suppliers in Japan revealed that all had, at one time or another, been visited by Toyota personnel who assisted in improving the suppliers' operations. On average, suppliers reported receiving 4.2 visits per year, and these visits lasted an average of 3.1 days.

The U.S. version of OMCD is called the Toyota Supplier Support Center (TSSC). TSSC was established in 1992 with the objective of "assisting North American suppliers to implement their own version of TPS."[10] TSSC's general manager, Hajime Ohba (formerly a member of OMCD in Japan), heads a staff that had grown to 20 consultants by 1998. During the past six years TSSC has received approximately 100 requests for assistance and has entered into 53 consultation projects. Toyota does not charge fees for its assistance but does demand that participating suppliers allow Toyota to bring other companies to see their operations when the project is completed. States TSSC consultant Lesa Nichols, "That's one of our requirements because if we take the time and effort to transfer the know-how, we need to be able to use the supplier's operations as a vehicle to help other suppliers."[11] This allows Toyota to develop some "showcase" or "best practice" suppliers that have successfully implemented various elements of the Toyota Production System, and to start the process of getting suppliers to open their operations to one another. (Suppliers can designate certain other areas of their plants—where Toyota has not provided assistance—as off-limits to visits in order to protect proprietary knowledge.)

To date, Toyota has found that know-how transfers with regard to TPS are extremely difficult and time consuming. Although the goal is to achieve success in 6 months, no project in the United States has been completed in less than 8 months, and most last at least 18 months. Hajme Ohba notes: "It takes a very long time and tremendous commitment to implement the Toyota Production System. In many cases it takes a total cultural and organizational change. Many U.S. firms have management systems that contradict where you need to go."[12]

Consequently, some of TSSC's consulting projects can be quite time and resource intensive. According to an executive at GHSP, a stamping supplier, "TSSC has been providing assistance to our plant for almost three years. One consultant practically lived at our plant for a year and became part of the plant family. In fact, we even threw him a baby shower when he had his first baby."[13]

By November 1997 TSSC had completed 31 projects with suppliers, with impressive results. On average, TSSC had assisted suppliers in achieving an average inventory reduction of 75 percent and an average increase in productivity or output per worker of 124 percent (see Figure 3.3). These data provide hard evidence that TSSC's knowledge-transfer processes substantially improve supplier performance. Of course, the real benefits are perhaps better understood by examining individual cases. For example, Continental Metal Specialty (CMS), a

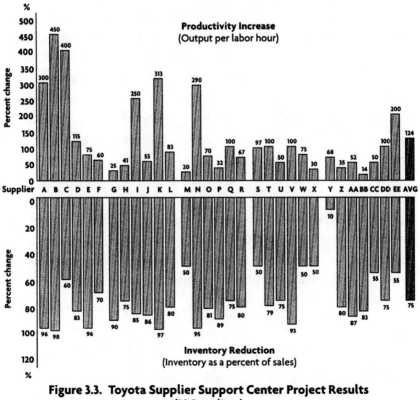

Figure 3.3. Toyota Supplier Support Center Project Results
(31 Suppliers)

(*Source:* TSSC, November 1997)

supplier of metal stampings (e.g., body brackets) has made dramatic improvements in productivity since becoming a Toyota supplier. The consulting process began when Toyota sent in people to teach CMS about "lean production principles." Then, CMS and Toyota examined CMS's production process to identify each step in the process and to flag those steps that were value added and those that were nonvalue added. Through this analysis CMS and Toyota identified four value-added processes (blanking, forming, welding, and painting the part) and twenty-six nonvalue-added process steps. They then focused their efforts on reconfiguring the production system to eliminate as many nonvalue-added steps as possible. One important change they made was to bring the welding step into the plant (previously it had been done in another plant) and position it next to the forming step. This allowed CMS to form/weld the pan in back-to-back steps, thereby eliminating twelve nonvalue-added steps. Over time, CMS has reduced their production process steps from 30 to 11, eliminating 19 nonvalue-added process steps in the production system. They also reduced set-up times from 2 hours to 12 to 15 minutes, and they cut their inventories on some parts to almost 1/10 that of previous levels, from 6000 parts to 606 parts. The benefits of learning were enormous. Stated CMS Chairman George Hommel, "We wouldn't be where we are now if we hadn't worked with Toyota. I'd say that 75 to 80 percent of all that we've learned from customers has come from Toyota."[14] It is important to note that Toyota does not ask for immediate price decreases or a portion of the savings from the improvements. However, suppliers claim that after the consulting engagement they often pass on some of the savings to Toyota due to a feeling of obligation. And even if they do not pass on the savings immediately, suppliers realize that some of the cost savings will need to be passed on to Toyota through price reductions at future annual or biennial price reviews.

Voluntary Study Groups (Jishuken)

OMCD facilitates knowledge sharing across suppliers in a way that is quite unique. In 1977 OMCD organized a group of roughly 55–60 of its key suppliers (providing over 80 percent of its parts in value) into "voluntary study groups" (*jishukenkyu-kai* or *jishuken*) for the purpose of assisting each other with productivity and quality improvements. Each supplier group consists of roughly five to eight suppliers, many of whom use similar production processes (e.g., stamping, welding, painting, etc.). Body suppliers are placed in one of two groups (groups I or II) and parts suppliers are placed in one of eight groups (groups A-H; see Figure 3.4). Toyota groups suppliers together based upon geographic proximity (suppliers that are physically close) and competition (direct competitors are not in the same group). Groups are usually reorganized every three years by Toyota to stimulate activity and maintain diversity of ideas. Each year the suppliers meet together with the responsible OMCD manager and consultants to determine a theme, or project, for the year. The basic idea is to help each other increase productivity in areas of common interest. Supplier executives that participate in *jishuken* activities are typically plant managers, assistant plant managers, and/or section managers (each member company usually has four to six people taking part in the activity).

After a theme is decided, the group sets a schedule to rotate from one supplier plant to the next to examine the processes in question and to jointly develop suggestions for improvement. The group focuses on one supplier plant for a period of four months, during which the pro-

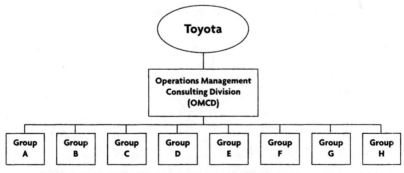

- Each group consists of 5–8 suppliers. Direct competitors are not in the same group. Group composition changes every 3 years to keep groups "fresh."
- Each group meets with Toyota to decide the theme (area of focus) for the year.
- The group visits each supplier's plant over a 4-month period, examining the processes and offering suggestions for improvement.
- OMCD visits frequently to give advice and monitor progress.
- Toyota organizes an annual meeting where each group presents the key learnings from the year's activities.

Figure 3.4. Toyota's Voluntary Study Groups (*jishuken*)

ject goes through four phases: preliminary inspection, diagnosis and experimentation, presentation, and follow-up and evaluation. During the first two months the plant's processes are evaluated, and the other suppliers visit as needed to examine the processes and offer suggestions for improvement. In effect, the supplier participants act as consultants to each other, drawing on their knowledge of manufacturing. A member of OMCD also visits every week or two to give advice and monitor progress. This allows Toyota to bring its expertise to bear to help solve supplier problems, and to benefit from what is being learned by suppliers. This adds to Toyota's stock of knowledge and allows OMCD to keep abreast of new ideas and applications of the Toyota Production System. This is valuable to both Toyota and the network because OMCD can transfer this knowledge to Toyota's internal operations or to other suppliers. At the end of the year Toyota organizes a conference where all of the *jishuken* groups gather to share what they have learned.

In 1994 Toyota replicated the *jishuken* concept in the United States by establishing its Plant Development Activity (PDA) core groups. Three groups were formed with 11 suppliers placed in each group. As with the supplier association, involvement was voluntary. The theme for the first year was "quality improvement" because, as Toyota's Chris Nielsen noted, "everyone agrees that they can improve quality."[15] Each PDA group member was asked to select a "demonstration line" within a plant as a place to experiment with new concepts. A schedule was developed to meet for one day each month at a supplier plant, during which Toyota personnel from the technical support group would implement key concepts at the demonstration line, and the group members would discuss ways to improve the line. The group would visit the same supplier for three months and then rotate to a new supplier.

The first year was successful enough that other suppliers requested the opportunity to join a PDA core group; Toyota added 15 suppliers and another PDA core group in 1995. However, some of the groups were experiencing difficulties because of markedly different skills and knowledge of TPS methods among suppliers. As Toyota technical support specialist Tom Fitzgibbons stated, "We tried high-skill and low-skill suppliers together, but sometimes it didn't work well because we had to keep stopping to explain basic concepts to the new suppliers."[16] Consequently, Toyota reorganized the groups in 1996 into four groups where skill level was also considered. The orange group included suppliers with strong TPS skills; the blue and green groups, those with mid-level skills; and the purple group consisted of less-experienced suppliers.

To be considered for participation in a PDA core group the supplier must be a member of BAMA for at least one year. Toyota claims that this requirement is necessary to assure assimilation into BAMA, top management commitment, and familiarity with the basic concepts of TPS (e.g., develop the requisite absorptive capacity within the supplier). U.S. plant managers report that the PDA core group activities have been extremely valuable. Stated one plant manager:

> We get blinded just like everyone else. When you bring a whole new set of eyes into your plant you learn a lot. You feel like you are getting beat up for the first few hours. We've made quite a few improvements. In fact, after the [PDA] group visits to our plant, we made more than 70 changes to the manufacturing cell.[17]

In fact, in a sample of 10 U.S. suppliers that I interviewed, each executive claimed that the PDA core group activities were more valuable to suppliers than BAMA. As one plant manager stated:

> I think BAMA is extremely valuable. But the PDA core group activities are even more valuable to us than BAMA. If I had to choose, I would definitely choose to be involved in the core groups rather than BAMA. We learn more that is useful in our daily operations.[18]

This comment suggests that the tacit knowledge acquired through the PDA core groups is perceived to be more valuable than the mostly explicit knowledge acquired through BAMA. A key reason that the PDA core group *jishusken* activities are particularly effective at tacit knowledge transfers is that they involve learning that is context specific (hands on and on site). For example, the plant manager from Kojima Press (a Japanese supplier of spoilers and body parts) described how they had acquired tacit knowledge through a *jishuken* project: "The *jishuken* projects were very helpful. Last year we were able to reduce our paint costs by 30 percent. This was possible due to a suggestion to lower the pressure on the paint sprayer and adjust the spray trajectory, thereby wasting less paint." Another plant manager noted: "We find more things that are useful visiting other suppliers' plants versus Toyota's plants; even simple things like how to best start our equipment. Suppliers' operations are more similar to ours." Like the supplier association, the *jishuken* and PDA core groups help create an identity for Toyota's extended enterprise, or the Toyota Group. As one supplier executive put it: "We're a member of the [blue] group. That means we are willing to do what we can to help other group members."

Problem-Solving Teams

Jishuken teams are designed to systematically diffuse knowledge that resides within network members to other members. However, in addition to *jishuken*, Toyota has a process of forming problem-solving teams designed to bring knowledge to bear in solving emergent problems within the network. For example, a supplier may be experiencing a quality problem where the root cause is not easily determined. In this case, Toyota's Quality Assurance Division (QAD) will set up a problem-solving team (including various Toyota divisions and possibly even other Toyota suppliers) to collectively bring their knowledge to bear to fix the quality problems. When established, the team defines the cause(s) of the supplier's quality problems and hands over responsibility for the problem-solving process to an appropriate division within Toyota. For example, if the team determines that the root of the supplier's quality problem is in the product design, Toyota's Design Engineering Division (which has already been involved in the problem-solving team) will be asked to take the lead in working with the supplier. In some cases, Toyota may determine that the relevant knowledge resides within a competitor of the supplier. In this case, Toyota may attempt to orchestrate a supplier-to-supplier knowledge transfer. Toyota has long maintained a two-vendor policy, and when the quality of one supplier is significantly inferior to another's, QAD may transfer knowledge from the better supplier to the inferior supplier based upon a negotiated agreement with both. In some rare cases, QAD will coordinate a visit by the inferior supplier to the superior supplier's plant.

I did not find this type of competitor supplier-to-supplier knowledge sharing between Toyota's suppliers in the United States. However, 70 percent of Toyota's U.S. suppliers reported that Toyota orchestrated trips to Japan during which they visited supplier plants, in some cases Japanese suppliers who were competitors producing the same component. As a supplier executive at Lucas Body Systems stated: "Toyota told us to work on cutting our changeover time from 2 hours to 30 minutes. I told them it was impossible. Then they sent me to visit a Japanese supplier in our same business that had changeover times of 15 minutes. I never would have believed it if I hadn't seen it with my own eyes." This type of exchange provides both incentives to improve as well as knowledge with regard to *how* to improve. Furthermore, according to some Toyota executives, upgrading the skills of the inferior supplier not only improves the quality of the weaker supplier but also stimulates long-term competition.

Interfirm Employee Transfers

The practice of interfirm employee transfers (*shukko*) in Japan is now well known. Some previous studies suggest that important reasons for *shukko* include helping large assemblers maintain control of suppliers and the opportunity to shed unwanted employees.[19] However, my interviews suggest that, at least in Toyota's case, *shukko* is also an important mechanism for transferring knowledge to suppliers. In a survey of 38 of Toyota's first-tier suppliers, I found that 11 percent of the suppliers' directors (*yakuin*) were former employees of Toyota (the figure was 23 percent for Toyota's affiliated suppliers, or suppliers in which Toyota owned some stock). Overall, Toyota transfers approximately 120–130 individuals per year to other firms in the value chain, most of whom go to suppliers.[20] Some of these transfers are permanent; others are temporary. For example, during one of my visits to Kojima Press, a supplier of spoilers and other body parts, I found that the assistant plant manager was a Toyota engineer on leave from Toyota for a two to three year assignment. He explained: "I am here to apply what I've learned at Toyota to help the plant manager run a more efficient plant. Also, by working at the supplier I can understand the supplier's perspective and what problems they experience." At another supplier, I interviewed a transferee who had been sent to the supplier to help it set up operations and accounting systems in the United States. This particular individual had worked in the automaker's U.S. operations and therefore had a knowledge of American accounting systems, which he was able to transfer to the supplier. In some cases the supplier had a need for particular skills or knowledge that members of its workforce did not possess. Consequently, it would make a request to the automaker (usually through purchasing to the personnel department) for someone with particular skills. The automaker would search within its organization and then offer someone to the supplier organization. Suppliers claimed that they had the right to refuse the person offered. However, given Toyota's importance as a customer, it is questionable as to whether this "right" is ever exercised. Regardless, these transfers are an important routine which fulfills a knowledge-transfer function. The transferred individuals bring with them a knowledge of Toyota's personnel, systems, and technology. Furthermore, the fact that individuals can be transferred across firm boundaries indicates that the unit of analysis for a job rotation is not the individual firm, but the extended enterprise. Thus, this practice further creates an identity for the extended enterprise. To date, these transfers only occur with Japanese suppliers in Japan.

Performance Feedback and Monitoring Processes

Finally, Toyota pushes suppliers to learn by providing frequent performance feedback and by monitoring whether or not suppliers implement new knowledge and technology. Toyota systematically offers feedback in a number of areas, including management, production costs, quality, and delivery. This feedback, in turn, motivates suppliers to improve. As one Toyota analyst observed:

> Without naming names the [performance] summary . . . enabled each supplier to see quite easily where the company stood in relation to other companies in the same line of business and in relation to all the other companies. This ranking of suppliers and its publication at an open meeting in a form that made it easy for

suppliers to compare themselves with others had the effect of stimulating a more competitive spirit among suppliers.[21]

In addition to regular performance feedback, Toyota also provides more detailed feedback on an ad hoc basis and occasionally conducts audits to monitor whether or not suppliers are implementing new processes. For example, the Quality Assurance Division visits suppliers on a rotating basis to ensure that quality systems and processes maintain the company's standard. The purchasing division identifies which suppliers it wants QAD to visit based upon an evaluation of the supplier's quality performance. Naturally, suppliers with a history of quality problems are more likely to be audited. During these audits, QAD writes a "quality problem report," which analyzes whether there might be chronic and fundamental problems in a supplier's production system. These audits also give QAD an opportunity to provide direct, on-site instruction to suppliers. In similar fashion, Toyota's cost-planning departments within both purchasing and engineering monitor suppliers' components costs. Suppliers identified as high cost would then be targeted for a visit from OMCD.

After offering instruction to suppliers, Toyota documents the changes that they are asked to make. They use this documentation later when monitoring the suppliers' processes. To illustrate, a U.S. supplier executive described how Toyota used this information to push his company to learn and improve.

> Toyota sent in a team of consultants to offer suggestions on how we could reduce our costs to meet the target cost. Their help was extremely valuable and we made some significant improvements. But after considerable effort we felt we would be unable to hit the target cost. So we visited the purchasing manager to ask for a price increase. After we made the request, the purchasing manager pulled out a file which had a list of the actions we were to take based upon the suggestions of their consultants. While pointing to the first item on the list, he asked, "Have you done this yet?" Fortunately we had and we responded positively. But then he proceeded to go through each item on the list. We could only answer "yes" to about two-thirds of the items. Then he said

politely, "When you have taken action on every item on this list
you won't need a price increase; but if you still think you do, come
back and we will discuss it."[22]

This supplier executive explained that while Toyota is generous in
offering assistance, they also expect results and countermeasures whenever the supplier does not meet performance expectations.

In summary, Toyota has created both an organizational unit
(OMCD) and a number of supporting processes designed to acquire,
store, and diffuse knowledge throughout its extended enterprise. These
processes facilitate both bilateral and multilateral transfers of explicit
and tacit knowledge. Recently, Toyota has taken an unprecedented step
to facilitate communication with and among suppliers. To signal the
importance of its suppliers, Toyota built a Supplier Center next to its
headquarters and technical center in Toyota City, Japan. The new five-
floor building, completed in 1998 to commemorate the fiftieth
anniversary of the *kyohokai*, has display rooms for suppliers' products
as well as meeting rooms to be used for suppliers. Thus, the building
is an extended enterprise building, not a Toyota building. The building represents not only Toyota's commitment to working closely with
its suppliers, but also demonstrates Toyota's awareness of the importance of communication among firms within its extended enterprise.

Evidence of Superior Learning
Among Toyota's U.S. Suppliers

Recently Toyota has transplanted to the United States the production
of the majority of its U.S.-sold vehicles. Furthermore, in part to meet
local content requirements, Toyota now buys more than 70 percent of
its parts (for U.S. plants) from U.S.-based suppliers. Thus, Toyota is
increasingly using the identical suppliers as its U.S. competitors. This
raises an interesting question: Can a firm that uses the identical suppliers as its competitors and purchases roughly similar inputs achieve
a competitive advantage through those suppliers? Traditional economic theory suggests that this would only be possible if the buying
firm can extract lower unit prices from suppliers due to greater rela-

tive bargaining power than its competitors.[23] However, in the United States Toyota has less relative bargaining power than its U.S. competitors due to lower unit volumes, or market share. If anything we would expect U.S. automakers to have a differential advantage.

Beyond bargaining power, the only other way that Toyota could possibly achieve competitive advantages through identical suppliers would be to provide assistance (knowledge and technology) to the supplier to improve the productivity of the supplier's operations that are dedicated to Toyota. However, if Toyota transfers valuable knowledge and technology to a particular U.S. supplier, what is to prevent the supplier from utilizing that knowledge in supplying products to Ford, GM, and Chrysler? Is it possible for suppliers to have different levels of productivity for different customers? Can Toyota still create competitive advantages through its supply chain even when it is not the dominant customer, and even when it is using the same suppliers as its competitors?

To examine this issue I surveyed Toyota's U.S. suppliers (the 97 suppliers in BAMA) to determine, first, the extent to which they engage in knowledge-sharing activities with Toyota and with their largest U.S. customer; and second, the extent to which the productivity of the supplier's operations (for the same type of components in the same plant) differs for Toyota versus the U.S. customer. By studying suppliers making similar parts for different customers it is possible to control for extraneous variation and focus on the specific processes by which those suppliers learn from Toyota versus their largest U.S. customer.

The findings were illuminating. First, I found that Toyota engages in more knowledge-sharing activities with its U.S. suppliers than do its Big Three competitors. Toyota sends personnel to visit the suppliers' plants to share technical information an average of 13 days each year, versus 6 days for Big Three customers. Further, because of their relationship with Toyota (and more specifically, due to the PDA core groups), suppliers visit, and are visited by, other suppliers for 34 days each year. In contrast, the suppliers report that the relationship with their largest U.S. customer (GM, Ford, Chrysler) results in only 6 days of knowledge exchanges with other suppliers. All of the plant managers reported receiving significantly more cost and quality assistance from Toyota. As the plant manager of a supplier of carpets and interior parts noted:

> We have received a great deal of knowledge from Toyota. Toyota provides the most training of any OEM. We have learned about in-sequence shipping, *kanban*, one-piece production, and standardized work. We have even learned some of Toyota's H/R related training philosophy and methods.[24]

Stated another plant manager: "With Toyota's help we redesigned our production process. We eliminated three forklifts by using wheels on carts to stack our product. We eliminated conveyor belts. We dramatically cut inventories. Ninety percent of everything we have learned from our customers, we've learned from Toyota."[25] Perhaps the most dramatic example was offered by the vice president of planning at a supplier of stamped parts, who stated:

> We reduced our process steps from 34 to 14, eliminating 20 non-value-added process steps from our production process. We reduced set-up times from 2 hours to 15 minutes, and we cut our inventory to almost 1/10 of previous levels.[26]

The plant managers I interviewed were unanimous in their opinion that Toyota provided more valuable assistance than their largest U.S. customer, despite that fact that, on average, they sold less than half the volume to Toyota.

Not surprisingly, I found that Toyota's knowledge-sharing practices resulted in a faster rate of learning at suppliers, which translated into higher productivity and quality (see Figure 3.5). More specifically, from 1990 to 1996 the typical supplier reduced its defects (in parts per million) by 84 percent for Toyota versus 46 percent for its largest Big Three customer. Similarly, on average suppliers reduced their inventories (as a percent of sales) by 35 percent in their operations devoted to Toyota versus only a 6 percent reduction for their largest Big Three customer. And finally, suppliers increased their labor productivity (sales per direct employee) by 36 percent for Toyota versus only a 1 percent increase for their largest Big Three customer. By 1996 suppliers had achieved 10 percent higher output per worker and had roughly 25 per-

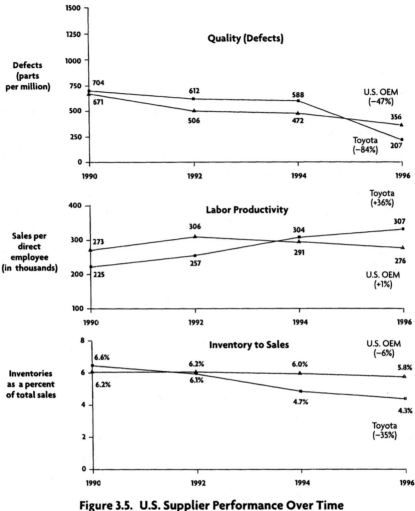

Figure 3.5. U.S. Supplier Performance Over Time
(For Toyota versus the Supplier's largest U.S. OEM)

Note: Percent change from 1990–1996 is in parenthesis

cent lower inventories on their manufacturing cells for Toyota compared to their largest U.S. customer. The suppliers also had 35 percent fewer defects (parts per million) for Toyota. These differences are amazing when one considers that these are differences *within the same supplier's plant.* My findings demonstrate that suppliers do, in some instances, have different levels of performance for different customers. But why doesn't the supplier replicate what they have learned from Toyota in their operations devoted to other customers?

Why Toyota's Learning Advantages Are Sustainable

We now turn to the question of why cost and quality differences may persist even within the same plant. Overall, one-third of the suppliers reported that they *did* transfer the knowledge acquired from Toyota to their manufacturing cells devoted to their largest U.S. customer. However, two-thirds of the plant managers reported that they did not. Their operations devoted to Toyota consistently produced higher quality products at lower cost (with fewer people and less inventories). To explore the reasons behind the productivity and quality differences, I conducted follow-up interviews with plant managers where within-plant differences in cost and quality persisted. In these exploratory interviews, the plant managers reported that they wanted to transfer the knowledge to other manufacturing cells, but they claimed they *could not*. They identified two key barriers to intraplant knowledge transfers.

External System Constraints

In some instances the plant manager reported being unable to transfer the knowledge employed in one manufacturing cell to another cell due to "system constraints" imposed by the customer. For example, customers sometimes dictate "production process requirements" to the supplier and simply do not allow the supplier to change the process. To illustrate, one supplier was required by its Big Three customer to use large (approximately four feet by six feet) reusable containers. When filled with components, these containers weighed 200–300 pounds. By comparison, Toyota had the supplier use small (two feet by three feet) reusable containers weighing 40 pounds when filled. This one difference immediately created a number of changes in the production process. The process for the Big Three customer required significantly more floor space due to the size of the containers. The supplier needed to purchase forklifts and hire forklift operators to move the containers. The large containers were more difficult to handle and keep clean, which affected product quality. The large containers also made it more difficult to label and sort products into a particular sequence for production at the assembler's facility. Because the large containers fit well into the Big Three assembler's system (which also used forklifts and lots of floor space), the customer would not allow the supplier to change the process. Thus, the supplier was unable to imitate the processes in the Toyota manufacturing cells because the supplier's operations represented one element or stage within the production network. The ability to change processes in that one element of the production network was constrained by that element's connections to other parts of the network. This provides further evidence that the production network is a critical unit of analysis for understanding competitive advantage.

Plant managers reported that constraints imposed by the customer were often considerable. A study by Wu and Liker (1999) illustrates how customer policies influence a supplier's ability to implement "lean" production techniques.[27] They found that suppliers are better able to keep inventories low in their Toyota manufacturing cells because Toyota provides more stable production forecasts that allow the supplier to more effectively level production. Toyota's production forecasts only fluctuated 3 percent during the final 3 days before production. In contrast, U.S. OEM volumes fluctuate dramatically, with Ford and GM's forecasts fluctuating by 20 percent during the final 3 days before production. In addition, U.S. OEMs are more likely to require that suppliers ship full trucks, thereby forcing suppliers to hold more inventories.

Suppliers also felt constrained because whenever they wanted to make a major process change they had to get approval from the customer. Because these approvals were time consuming and difficult to obtain, many times plant managers simply avoided the hassle. Furthermore, to make significant changes to a manufacturing cell often requires considerable down time. The other customer must allow the supplier the down time necessary to make the changes and be willing to accept the risk that the new processes will have some bugs that will need to be worked out.

Internal Process Rigidities

In addition to facing external system constraints, some suppliers did not transfer the knowledge gained from Toyota due to process rigidities in the layout of the manufacturing cells for their U.S. customer. In particular, they were much less likely to transfer the knowledge when the manufacturing cells for the Big Three customer had a high level of automation or large capital investment in heavy equipment. In some cases large machines and equipment were bolted or cemented into the floor, there was trenching in the floor, or the utilities were hardwired to the machines. Consequently, there were internal process rigidities that increased the costs of making the transfer. The manufacturing cells for the U.S. customers were designed as static systems and thus were simply not flexible to change, or the cost of the change was viewed as prohibitive. As one plant manager reported: "When you invest in automation, you do everything you can to run that job for as long as you can. When you have to change a highly automated process you have a devil of a time. It just never works." In contrast, Toyota's production network is designed as a dynamic system. The flexibility to modify the system is built into the processes and procedures. This may explain why suppliers had relatively low rates of productivity improvement for their U.S. customers. These internal process rigidities resulted in plant managers either choosing not to make the change or waiting until the vehicle model changed before implementing a new process. Thus, at the very least, internal process rigidities created a significant time lag before the new processes were implemented.

Finally, it is important to recognize that both the internal process rigidities and the external system constraints created risks for suppliers who wanted to transfer the knowledge. For example, the president of one supplier argued:

> The Toyota Production System is a very fragile system which requires constant attention. One person can make a minor change and it can mess up the whole system. This is a real problem in dealing with [our U.S. customer]. Any time we want to change the process, we must follow a set of bureaucratic rules. Anytime you deal with the customer's bureaucracy it's a real problem. And if you make a change that causes a problem, and you've not followed their procedure exactly, then you have a huge liability. If you cause a recall, or even if they think you caused a

recall, it could put you out of business. And if you shut down their plant they charge you $30,000 a minute. Sometimes it's just not worth the risk.[28]

Thus, some suppliers did not transfer the knowledge because of the huge risks associated with failure.

In summary, Toyota is able to generate competitive advantages through knowledge sharing in its extended enterprise even when it uses the identical suppliers as its competitors. It is unclear to what extent Toyota realizes lower costs as a result of helping suppliers. It is possible (but unlikely) that suppliers appropriate all of the gains from the cost assistance received. Without specific component price information for each customer (which suppliers were unwilling to provide), I cannot answer this question. However, Toyota clearly realizes a quality advantage in the marketplace as a result of these knowledge-sharing initiatives. Because Toyota's suppliers have 35 percent fewer defects, Toyota's vehicles also have fewer defects. This is extremely valuable in differentiating Toyota's vehicles from its competitors. It is worth noting that my quality findings are consistent with data from J.D. Power and Associates, whose studies consistently indicate that Toyota vehicles have roughly 30–40 percent fewer problems per 100 vehicles than those of Big Three automakers.[29] I estimate the cost to Toyota of orchestrating these various knowledge-sharing initiatives (OMCD, TSSC, supplier association, etc.) to be roughly $50–100 million per year. For a $100-billion company like Toyota, this is a relatively small amount to pay to help create a significant quality advantage.

Conclusion

In this chapter I examined how competitive advantage can be created through superior knowledge-sharing processes within the extended enterprise. I first explained why perfectly increasing returns with regard to knowledge gives firm networks substantial learning advantages over individual firms. I described six key knowledge-sharing routines employed by Toyota, most of which are not employed by Toyota's

U.S. competitors. I also demonstrated that it is possible for a firm to create collaborative advantages through its supplier network even when that same network is used by competitors. My research convincingly demonstrates that automakers can achieve competitive advantage by developing superior routines to transfer knowledge to, and among, suppliers within the value chain. However, without trust in the extended enterprise, knowledge sharing would vanish and transaction costs would escalate. In the next chapter I explore how Toyota builds trust, and generates value from trust, in its extended enterprise.

4

Creating Trust in the Extended Enterprise

Interactions—the searching, coordinating, and monitoring that people and firms do when they exchange goods, services, or ideas—account for over a third of economic activity in the United States.

—Report by McKinsey & Company

Trust is critical. It's hard to place a value on it. But without it, you waste lots of time in negotiations and trying to get a bargaining advantage. And forget sharing any information that you don't have to.

—Sales vice president, U.S. supplier

Like motherhood and apple pie, trust is one of life's indisputable virtues. Indeed, the management literature is full of testimonials about companies that claim they benefited by building trust with suppliers or customers. But does trust really pay off in significant bottom-line results, or does this feel-good approach only bring marginal benefits? Most "research" on trust is anecdotal, with little evidence of hard economic benefits. And even if the benefits are significant, how does a company best go about building trust within its extended enterprise?

My research—some of the first empirical work on a large sample of 453 supplier-automaker relationships—demonstrates that supplier-buyer trust can be a valuable economic asset that pays off in significant bottom-line results. More specifically, trust is valuable within the extended enterprise because it:

- lowers transaction costs (which are significant, as I will soon demonstrate),[1]
- leads to superior knowledge sharing,[2] and
- facilitates investments in dedicated assets.[3]

In this chapter I examine the costs of mistrust and provide strong evidence that trust lowers transaction costs throughout the extended enterprise. I also discuss the important role that trust plays in increasing both information sharing and investments in dedicated assets between suppliers and automakers. Finally, I examine the issue of how firms can develop trusting relationships within the extended enterprise. Surprisingly, I find that Toyota's ability to develop trust with suppliers is not based primarily on personal relationships between Toyota and its suppliers. Nor is it based on the stock ownership it holds in its *keiretsu* suppliers. Rather, trust between large organizations is based on each firm's institutionalized processes for dealing with external firms.

Defining Trust

I define *trust* as one party's confidence that the other party in the exchange relationship will fulfill its promises and commitments and will not exploit its vulnerabilities.[4] This confidence would be expected to emerge in situations where the trustworthy party makes good-faith efforts to behave in accordance with prior commitments, makes adjustments (e.g., as market conditions change) in ways perceived as fair by the exchange partner, and does not take advantage of an exchange partner even when the opportunity is available. Thus, my definition characterizes interfirm trust as a construct based on three components: reliability, fairness, and goodwill.

Conceptually, organizations are not able to trust each other; trust has its basis in individuals. Trust can only be placed by one individual in another individual or in a group of individuals, such as a partner organization. However, individuals in an organization may share an orientation toward individuals within another organization. From this perspective, *interorganizational trust* describes the extent to which there is a collectively held "trust orientation" by organizational members toward another firm.[5] It is also important to note that the need for trust only arises in a risky situation, because without some vulnerability, there is no need to trust.[6] Supplier-automaker relationships are fraught with risk and vulnerabilities—which is why trust is particularly important in this industry.

The automobile is a complex product with thousands of components that must work together as a system. Components are often tailored to specific models, and as a result suppliers must make dedicated (automaker-specific) investments in people, plant, tools, equipment, and so forth.[7] Since these investments are not easily redeployable to other uses, suppliers are at risk if their automaker customers behave opportunistically. For example, after a supplier has made an investment in a dedicated asset, the automaker may try to renegotiate a contract, threatening to switch to another supplier if the price is not lowered. Furthermore, the auto industry is characterized by a high degree of market uncertainty,[8] which increases both the risks associated with transacting as well as the importance of information sharing.[9] For example, the automaker may expect to sell 100,000 units of a particular model and request that the supplier make the necessary investments to produce parts for 100,000 units. But due to market uncertainty, the automaker may only be able to sell 50,000 or 75,000 units, thereby placing the supplier in the difficult situation of having invested in assets that are not needed. The supplier will lose money on this investment unless it can trust the automaker to help it recoup its investment (or, alternatively, the supplier must anticipate the potential problem and write provisions for it in a legal contract). Unfortunately, many potential problems are difficult to foresee and, therefore, write in a contract.

Differences in Automaker Trustworthiness

Automakers differ in the degree to which they are perceived as trustworthy by suppliers. I asked supplier executives a number of questions (on the automaker's reliability, fairness, and goodwill) to assess how much they trusted the various automakers. The results were interesting, though perhaps not surprising given that numerous trade and

popular journals have reported that suppliers are less likely to trust
automakers that use hardball procurement strategies. The results,
reported in Table 4.1, show that Toyota is the automaker most trusted
by suppliers, meaning that Toyota is most likely to follow through on
commitments, most likely to treat the supplier in ways perceived as
fair, and least likely to take advantage of a supplier when the supplier
is vulnerable. Nissan was the next most trusted automaker, followed
by Chrysler, Ford, and finally General Motors. Interestingly, the survey results also indicate that Toyota had developed significantly higher
levels of trust with U.S. suppliers than U.S. automakers. Thus, trust
can be developed relatively quickly with foreign suppliers in a new
country. (The question of how Toyota was able to quickly develop

**Table 4.1. Automaker Differences in Trust, Transaction Costs,
and Information Sharing**

	Chrysler	Ford	GM	Nissan	Toyota
1. *Supplier Trust in the Automaker*					
Extent to which automaker can be trusted to treat supplier fairly	5.4	5.0	3.2	6.1	6.4
If given the chance, extent to which automaker might try to take unfair advantage of supplier	2.9	3.6	5.4	1.8	1.4
Automaker has a reputation for fairness among supplier community	5.2	4.8	2.8	5.7	6.3
2. *Transaction Costs*					
Dollar value of goods procured per procurement employee	$5.7m	$5.3m	$1.6m	$9.6m	$12.6m
3. *Information Sharing*					
Extent to which supplier shares confidential information	4.3	3.6	2.6	5.4	6.1
4. *Assistance Giving*					
Automaker shares information to assist supplier with cost reduction	2.0	2.0	2.1	3.3	3.3
Automaker shares information to assist supplier with quality improvement	3.1	3.7	2.2	3.5	3.7
Automaker shares information to assist supplier with delivery and inventory management	2.5	2.2	1.9	2.8	3.8
5. *Re-win Rate* Percent of time the supplier re-wins the part business at a model change	80%	78%	58%	90%	92%

* 1 =Not at all; 4=To some extent; 7=To a very great extent trusting relationships with U.S. suppliers is an important one that I will address shortly.) It is important to point out that these differences in trustworthiness between Toyota and U.S. automakers are statistically significant: however, the more important question is whether or not these differences are *substantive*, at least in the sense that they impact the economic performance of these firms.

Trust Lowers Transaction Costs

Historically, a firm has been viewed by economists (and most executives) as a "production function." Consequently, the firm with the most efficient, or lowest cost, production function would win in the marketplace. The value chain reflected the combined production functions of all of the firms that engaged in exchanges, from "upstream" raw materials to "downstream" final assembly. Theoretically, the value chain comprising firms with the combined low-cost production functions would produce the final assembled product at the lowest total cost. However, recent work in economics has recognized that the productivity of a value chain or extended enterprise is a function of *both* production costs and transaction costs. *Transaction costs* involve all of the costs associated with conducting exchanges between firms. Transaction costs take many everyday forms—management meetings, conferences, phone conversations, sales calls, bidding rituals, reports, memos—but their underlying economic purpose is always to enable the exchange of goods, services, or ideas. The sales, marketing, distribution, procurement, logistics, and legal functions within most companies tend to represent a firm's investment in transacting with other parties.

Not only have we begun to recognize that transaction costs exist, but we are beginning to realize that in some industrial settings transaction costs are significant. Indeed, Nobel Prize winner Douglas North estimates that transaction costs may represent as much as 35–40 percent of the costs associated with economic activity.[10] As noted at the opening of this chapter, a study by strategy consultant McKinsey & Company found that the costs of exchanging goods and services, including search, coordination, and monitoring costs, account for over a third of economic activity in the United States. The McKinsey study also determined that "at an economy level, interactions [similar to trans-action costs] represent as much as 51 percent of labor activity in the United States—the equivalent of over a third of GDP."[11] If true, or even if both Douglas North and McKinsey & Company have overestimated transaction costs by a factor of two, then the extended enterprise that achieves the lowest transaction costs is likely to realize advantages in the marketplace.

Transaction costs can be divided into four separate costs: search costs, contracting costs, monitoring costs, and enforcement costs.[12] *Search costs* include the costs of gathering information to identify and evaluate potential trading partners—to find the right party with which to exchange. *Contracting costs* refer to the costs associated with nego-tiating and writing an agreement or legal contract. *Monitoring costs* refer to the costs associated with monitoring the agreement to ensure that each party fulfills the predetermined set of obligations. *Enforce-ment costs* refer to the costs associated with ex post bargaining (bar-gaining after the contract has been signed) and sanctioning a trading partner that does not perform according to the agreement.

In general, trust is more effective than legal contracts (third-party enforcement mechanisms) at minimizing transaction costs for a num-ber of reasons. First, search costs are lower for the buyer because the buyer does not need to comparison shop in order to be sure they are getting a fair deal. Assuming the supplier is relatively efficient, the buyer can trust that the price and quality offered by the supplier are fair. Second, negotiation and contracting costs are reduced because the exchange partners are more likely to openly share information and trust that payoffs will be divided fairly. Consequently, exchange part-ners do not have to bear the cost, or time, of specifying every detail of the agreement in a contract. Further, contracts are less effective than trust at controlling opportunism because they fail to anticipate all forms of cheating that may occur. Third, trust lowers monitoring costs because trust relies on self-monitoring rather than external or third-party monitoring. Exchange partners do not need to invest in costly monitoring mechanisms to ensure contract fulfillment and to docu-ment infractions to the satisfaction of a third party (e.g., court). Fourth, trust lowers the costs associated with changing the nature of the agreement, thereby allowing exchange partners to adjust the agreement "on the fly" to respond to unforseen market changes.[13] Finally, trust is superior to contracts at minimizing transaction costs over the long run because trust is not subject to the time limitations of contracts. Contracts are typically written for a fixed duration and, in effect, *depreciate* because they only provide protection during the designated length of the agreement. At the end of the contract duration the alliance partners need to write a new contract. Trust allows suppliers and automakers to avoid the costs of re-contracting. In fact, rather than depreciating, trust may *appreciate* over time, in the sense that trust usually increases with increased familiarity and interaction.[14]

One of the goals of my research has been to test whether or not trust does indeed reduce transaction costs—and to see whether this creates substantive economic value. I used two measures of transaction costs to try to determine the costs of mistrust. First, I asked suppliers to estimate how much of their face-to-face communication time with automakers involved negotiating a price or contract (bargaining before the contract is signed) or assigning blame for problems in the course of transacting (haggling after the contract is signed). This percentage is shown in Figure 4.1, along with each automaker's average score for supplier trust on the three trust submeasures (from Table 4.1). The results show that when supplier trust is high, transaction costs are low.

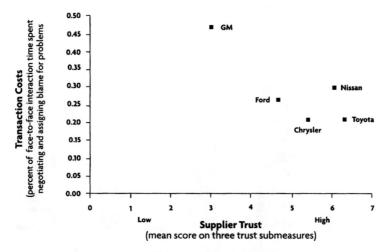

Figure 4.1. Trust Lowers Transaction Costs

More specifically, the most trusted automakers, Toyota and Chrysler, spent only about 21 percent of their face-to-face interaction time negotiating contracts and prices and assigning blame for problems. By comparison, General Motors spent 47 percent of its face-to-face interaction time on non-productive, transaction-oriented activities (see Figure 4.2). As a result, GM and its suppliers need to invest in 50 percent more face-to-face contact time in order to get the same number of hours of productive work time. As one supplier executive observed:

> We spend considerably more time with GM on non-productive activities. Because they bid more frequently, we have to spend a lot more time preparing bids and responding to requests for information. And if we win the bid, we are more likely to want to spell out the details of our agreement in a legal contract. It's costly but it helps protect us and also helps to make sure there are no misunderstandings down the road.[15]

While these differences in transaction costs may not be solely attributed to trusting relations between the firms, the fact that Toyota and Chrysler were twice as productive in their face-to-face interactions with suppliers when compared to General Motors is significant.

To further confirm that trust lowers transaction costs, I obtained another measure of each automaker's transaction costs based on more objective data. I obtained from each automaker the total number of

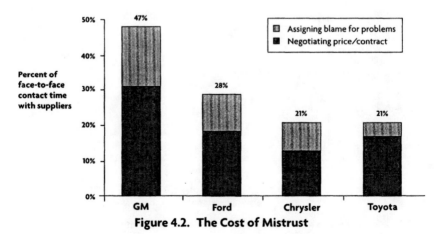

Figure 4.2. The Cost of Mistrust

employees in their procurement functions (including management, purchasing agents/buyers, lawyers, and support staff), as well as the total value of goods purchased. By dividing the number of procurement employees by the value of the goods purchased, I arrived at a rough estimate of the efficiency of each automaker's purchasing function. This is expressed as the dollar value of goods (parts) purchased per procurement employee. I believe this is a reasonably accurate measure of the relative transaction costs incurred by each automaker because the procurement staff is responsible for: searching for new suppliers, contracting with suppliers, monitoring supplier performance, and enforcing performance. Thus, this measure is a reasonable proxy for the relative transaction costs incurred by automakers. Not surprisingly, I found this measure to be highly correlated with the previous measure of transaction costs.[16]

When I plot this measure of procurement (transaction) costs for each automaker, along with the automaker's trustworthiness score, I find a very strong correlation between trust and procurement costs (see Figure 4.3).[17] The least-trusted automaker, General Motors, incurred procurement costs that were more than twice those of Chrysler and Ford, and almost six times higher than Toyota. When asked why GM had so many purchasing personnel and so many suppliers, one GM executive responded: "Our purchasing activities are huge and extensive. Most activities have been geared to making sure

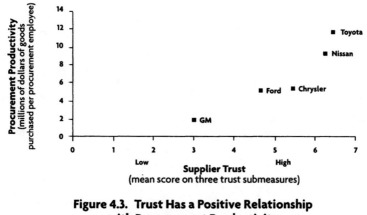

Figure 4.3. Trust Has a Positive Relationship with Procurement Productivity

we don't get stung by an unscrupulous supplier out there."[18] Although there are undoubtedly a number of factors that will influence an automaker's procurement efficiency, my research shows that trust is clearly an important factor.

In summary, supplier-automaker relationships with higher levels of trust had substantially lower transaction costs. Given the magnitude of the differences (and the fact that transaction costs are not trivial), the savings realized as a result of trusting relationships in the extended enterprise are large enough to be a real source of competitive advantage.

Trust Increases Knowledge Sharing

In addition to lowering transaction costs, trust has a profound influence on information sharing in supplier-buyer relationships. Not surprisingly, when suppliers trust their automaker customer they are more likely to share information with regard to product designs, technology, costs, manufacturing processes, and so forth. I asked suppliers to report on the extent to which they shared confidential information with their automaker customer. The results, reported in Figure 4.4, show that suppliers are much more likely to share confidential information with automakers they trust, notably Toyota, Nissan, and Chrysler. This finding was echoed in interviews with supplier executives, who claimed

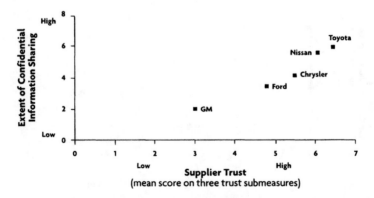

Figure 4.4. Trust Increases Confidential Information Sharing with the Automaker

that they were much more likely to bring new product designs and proprietary technologies to trustworthy automakers. Stated one supplier executive:

> We are much more likely to bring a new product design to Chrysler than to General Motors. The reason is simple. General Motors has been known to take our proprietary blueprints and send them to our competitors to see if they can make the part at lower cost. They claim they are simply trying to maintain competitive bidding. But because we can't trust them to treat us fairly, we don't take our new designs to them. We take them to Chrysler because we have learned that we can trust Chrysler.[19]

Suppliers are also much more likely to openly share information about their problems and request assistance when necessary. Most Toyota suppliers claimed that they would be willing to open their factories to Toyota consultants because they believed that these consultants possessed knowledge that could be truly valuable to their plants, and, just as important, because they trusted Toyota to offer the assistance without demanding an immediate price cut in return for cost improvements. In contrast, many General Motors suppliers indicated that they would prefer *not* to have General Motors' consultants come to their plants. Indeed, GM has sent such consultants (called PICOS teams) to suppliers to help them with their productivity. But they have had a very different reception, largely because suppliers do not trust GM. As described by one supplier executive:

> We don't want a PICOS team in our plant. I don't want them poking around our plant. They will just find the "low hanging fruit"—the stuff that's relatively easy to see and fix. We all have things in our plants that we know need to be fixed. They'll just come in, see it, and ask for a price decrease. We'd prefer to find it ourselves and keep all of the savings.[20]

Stated another supplier executive: "We allowed a PICOS team into our plant. They stayed for about a week and did make a few useful suggestions. Then we received a letter demanding a price decrease based upon the projected 'savings' from their suggestions."[21]

Thus, even though suppliers may be able to learn something from GM, they are reluctant to accept assistance or share any information because they do not trust GM or its motives (which they view as fully self-interested). The result is that GM may try to do the same things to help suppliers as Toyota, but due to a lack of trust it is not interpreted in a positive light.

In summary, trust unleashes the awesome power of information and knowledge, particularly valuable knowledge that may be viewed as proprietary by the supplier. This is important because the supplier's new designs and innovations may be critical in helping the buyer to differentiate its product in the marketplace.

Trust Increases Investments in Dedicated Assets

In Chapter 2 I discussed how investments in dedicated assets can enhance productivity in the production network.[22] However, investments in dedicated assets also create the potential for opportunism because these investments are not easily redeployable to other uses.[23] For example, suppose you are the president of a supplier, and a particular automaker builds a plant in Mexico and asks you to build a dedicated plant nearby. The automaker correctly argues that by building a plant nearby the two companies can realize inventory and transportation cost savings. Do you build the plant? Not unless you have strong assurances that the automaker will not try to take advantage of you down the road, perhaps by trying to renegotiate a contract. Thus, in order for the supplier to willingly make investments in dedicated assets, it must trust that the customer will not behave opportunistically. This is a real concern for suppliers, who do not want to make any investments that are not fully compensated during the term of the legal contract.[24] If the supplier does not trust the automaker, it may simply refuse to make dedicated investments that could create economic value. GM suppliers, in particular, reported an unwillingness to make investments in dedicated assets. This is a problem that is not confined to the automotive industry. Indeed, in a study of suppliers in a particular engineering field in the United Kingdom, Bruce Lyons found that 60 percent of the suppliers claimed that they were not utilizing the optimal level of dedicated asset investments with their main customer.[25] Why would a supplier consciously choose not to make the optimal investments in dedicated assets? The answer is that these suppliers were unwilling to expose themselves to the risk of being opportunistically exploited. In the absence of trust, suppliers will be very reluctant to make productivity-enhancing investments in assets that are dedicated to a particular customer.

The Determinants of Trust

Now that I have established that trust can create significant economic value by lowering transaction costs and increasing knowledge sharing, let us turn our attention to the issue of how to build trust within the extended enterprise. I previously argued that interfirm trust refers to a trust orientation by a group of individuals in one organization toward a group of individuals in another organization. This is different from interpersonal trust, which is trust between two individuals in two organizations. It is possible to have instances of interpersonal trust between organizations without having interorganizational trust. Let me explain.

I previously showed that U.S. suppliers trust Toyota more than they trust U.S. automakers. The question of how Toyota was able to quickly develop trusting relationships with U.S. suppliers is an important one. Certainly there was less time for U.S. suppliers to develop personal relationships with Toyota personnel compared to their long-standing relationships with U.S. automakers. And one would expect language and cultural differences to create barriers to building trust. Furthermore, Toyota has no stock ties in U.S. suppliers like they do with many of their Japanese suppliers. So what is going on here? The comment of a U.S. supplier executive, when asked why he trusted Toyota more than U.S. automakers, sheds light on this issue.

> We cannot trust U.S. automakers as much as Toyota because whenever they bring in new management, we get a whole new set of procurement rules and policies. The rules of the game are constantly changing. With Toyota, we don't seem to have the same problems because their policies and personnel are consistent and stable.[26]

This executive reported, as did many supplier executives, that the rules and policies at U.S. automakers (particularly GM and Ford) were unpredictable and inconsistent. The consequence of frequent changes in purchasing management and policies is that suppliers realize that implicit, and even explicit, promises made by the automaker may be broken when new management arrives. In short, the suppliers do not trust that the U.S. automaker's *processes* for working with suppliers will be fair and consistent. A second supplier executive illustrated another dimension of the difference between interpersonal and interorganizational trust.

> It's not that I don't trust the person sitting across from me at General Motors. In fact, I may feel more comfortable with him than his Japanese counterpart at Toyota. I may trust him completely. But what I don't trust is that he will be sitting there a year from now. U.S. automakers are constantly rotating their people through purchasing. And even if he's there, he may have to play by a new set of rules.[27]

Thus, U.S. suppliers claimed that their trust in Toyota was not based on greater interpersonal trust, but rather greater trust in the fairness, stability, and predictability of Toyota's routines and processes. I refer to this as *process-based trust*. I have found that process-based trust is critical for creating a trust orientation between individuals in two large organizations.

Process-based trust differs from interpersonal trust because the supplier's trust orientation toward the automaker is not based on personal relationships, but rather on a set of institutionalized processes and routines employed at the automaker. The "boundary-spanning" person (e.g., in procurement or engineering) at the automaker behaves in a trustworthy manner because the organizational culture and processes demand that someone in his or her particular role behave in a trustworthy manner. Thus, the automaker is viewed as trustworthy when it has institutionalized a set of practices and routines for dealing with a partner organization that transcend the influence of the individual boundary spanner. Process-based trust recognizes that interorganizational trust may be built upon impersonal structures, processes, and routines that create a stable context for exchange. Individuals may come and go at the two organizations, but the trust orientation will not be affected because trust is not based on individual relationships.

Assuming that trust is based more on processes than people, this raises the question of what processes are key to building trust. Through my interviews and surveys of suppliers, I have identified a number of practices that are important in developing trust within the extended enterprise.

Supplier-Selection Processes
That Demonstrate Commitment

One of the key processes that can either foster, or destroy, supplier trust is the process used by the automaker to select a supplier for a new vehicle model. In some instances, buyers use a competitive bidding process whereby incumbents are not given any advantage in ensuing rounds, regardless of past performance. This is an arm's-length competitive bidding process typically used by U.S. companies such as General Motors. In other instances, automakers may select suppliers based upon their track record for performance and give incumbents the first opportunity to garner new business. This is a selection process that favors incumbents and is often said to typify Japanese supplier-buyer relationships (though some U.S. firms, notably Chrysler, are increasingly using this approach). My research shows that the competitive bidding process fosters mistrust and that automakers who aggressively use competitive bidding are *always* viewed as less trustworthy. According to suppliers, the competitive bidding system immediately creates an adversarial relationship with the automaker because the exchange relationship is set up as a zero-sum game. The automaker may further exacerbate the problem by using the price comparisons to back up threats to switch business away unless it gets a better deal. As a result, suppliers conclude that the automaker views them as expendable and cares little for their profitability or survival. In short, the competitive bidding process does not make the suppliers feel like they are an important member of the extended enterprise. Instead they are a temporary member of a value chain—and the suppliers know they had better make as much profit on the current piece of business as possible because there are no future guarantees. Thus, competitive bidding practices do not foster trust between automakers and their suppliers.

In contrast, Toyota does not choose suppliers by competitive bid, but rather selects suppliers for new models based upon their track record for performance and previous history with Toyota. If a supplier has manufactured the braking system or air conditioner on the previous Toyota Camry or Corolla, then there is a better than 90 percent chance that it will "re-win" the business at the model change. Of course, the ability to re-win the business at the model change will depend on the supplier's performance (on cost, quality, delivery, etc.) on the previous model and the ability to meet the target cost (I will discuss this in greater detail in the next chapter). But if the supplier performs well, it knows it can count on getting the business on the next model. Supplier trust emerges under these conditions because the supplier can count on a long-term relationship and it knows that there is a low probability that the automaker will switch (perhaps opportunistically) the business to a competitor.[28] In the language of game theory, giving incumbents an advantage in the next round serves as a signal to the supplier that the automaker is playing a long-run "cooperative equilibrium" or a "repeated game." Repeated exchange is particularly important to the development of supplier trust in situations where suppliers have invested in dedicated assets. Under these conditions, an automaker's willingness to stay with the same supplier is interpreted by the supplier as a signal of commitment and trustworthiness.

To demonstrate the relationship between supplier selection processes and trust, I asked suppliers to provide their historical experience with regard to re-winning the contract when there was a model change. In the automotive industry, the model change is a natural time for buyers to reevaluate suppliers and make a change if deemed appropriate. Automakers who use competitive bidding and frequently change suppliers will have a lower re-win rate than automakers who have selection processes that favor incumbents. The results, shown in Figure 4.5, show a strong correlation between an automaker's re-win

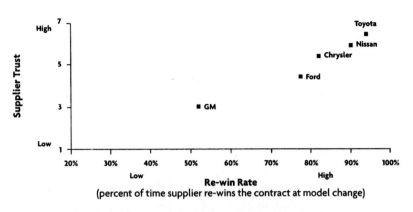

**Figure 4.5. Trust Increases as an Automaker's
Re-win Rate Increases**

rate and its trustworthiness. Suppliers to GM reported that they only re-win the business 58 percent of the time at contract renewal. Thus, they have had almost a 50 percent chance of getting thrown out at the model change. These suppliers also report relatively low trust in General Motors. In contrast, Toyota suppliers report that they have experienced a 92 percent re-win rate. Suppliers to Toyota have a high expectation of a long-term, continuous relationship and feel that they are an important member of Toyota's extended enterprise. Not surprisingly, they view Toyota as a much more trustworthy customer.

Free Assistance to the Supplier

A second way that Toyota builds suppliers' trust is by helping them improve. In the previous chapter, I described how Toyota sends its consultants to transfer knowledge to suppliers to help them improve productivity and quality. In addition, I found that this was an important method of building trust. U.S. suppliers reported that they received significantly more assistance from Toyota that they did from their U.S. customers. Indeed, some U.S. suppliers claimed that they received more help from Toyota than they felt they deserved given their short-term relationship. As the vice president of planning for a supplier of plastic interior parts stated:

I couldn't believe it, but Toyota sent approximately two to four consultants *every day* for a period of three to four months as we attempted to implement Toyota Production System concepts in a new plant. They gave us a valuable gift [the Toyota Production System].... Naturally we feel indebted towards Toyota and view them as a special customer; they sincerely want to help us improve.[29]

This type of assistance-giving behavior on the part of Toyota was a catalyst for creating a norm of reciprocal obligation and trust.

The importance of "gift exchange" in creating trust and reciprocity in exchange relationships has long been argued by a distinguished line of anthropologists and sociologists.[30] For example, in a seminal article sociologist Alvin Gouldner argued that a norm of reciprocity begins with a "starting mechanism," which may take the form of a gift or other acts of assistance.[31] Suppliers interpret Toyota's assistance-giving behavior as a signal of goodwill and commitment—an indication that Toyota is genuinely concerned with the well being of the supplier. In effect, the assistance is viewed by the supplier as a signal that Toyota does not have opportunistic intent.

To examine the relationship between assistance giving and trust, I asked suppliers to report on the extent to which they received various types of assistance from automakers. For example, I asked: "To what extent has the automaker provided assistance that has helped you reduce manufacturing costs?" and "To what extent has the automaker provided assistance that has helped you improve quality?" Suppliers reported on the extent to which they had received assistance on a seven-point scale, with 1 meaning "not at all," 4 meaning "to some extent," and 7 meaning "to a very great extent." I then averaged the assistance scores to get an overall measure of the extent to which each automaker provided assistance to suppliers. The relationship between automaker assistance and supplier trust is shown in Figure 4.6. Again, the results show that Toyota provides the most assistance and is also the most trusted automaker. (A regression analysis confirms a strong correlation between assistance and trust.) Clearly, providing assistance without requesting an immediate payback is one way to build trust within the extended enterprise.

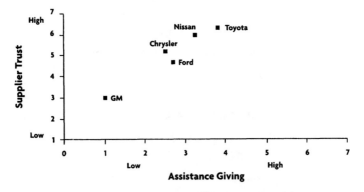

**Figure 4.6. Trust Increases as Automakers Provide Assistance
to Suppliers**

Stable, Long-Term Employment

Much has been written about the Japanese practice of long-term
employment within one firm.[32] Its importance in developing trust
between individuals across firms cannot be ignored. Although I have
tried to highlight that trust between large organizations can be, and
often is, based upon processes rather than personal relationships, stability of employment and relationships also results in stability of
processes. Further, trust is greatest among companies when *both* interpersonal and process-based trust exist. In Japan, trust between Toyota
and its suppliers is higher than in the United States because process-
based trust is combined with interpersonal trust. There are strong personal relations between the purchasing manager of Toyota and the
manager or owner of a supplier. The importance of these personal
relationships should not be underestimated. Naturally, you are more
likely to trust someone with whom you have done business for a long
period of time. It is much harder to build a trusting relationship with
someone if you think they will be gone in six months, as happens in
many U.S. companies. Hence, because Toyota's people can develop
long-standing relationships with their counterparts at the supplier, it
is not surprising that Toyota has been able to develop significantly
greater trust within its extended enterprise.

Both U.S. and Japanese suppliers contend that Toyota is more trustworthy than U.S. automakers due to its lifetime employment and pro-motion-from-within policies, which foster stability in personnel and policies. To test these assertions about stability, I examined employee tenure in two Japanese (Toyota and Nissan) and two U.S. (Ford and Chrysler) automakers. I surveyed a random sample of 100 U.S. and 100 Japanese purchasing and engineering employees (of roughly the same age) to determine the average tenure of employment. I found that pur-chasing and engineering employees at Toyota and Nissan had been with their employer for an average of 16.2 years, while their counterparts at Ford and Chrysler had only been at their company for 8.8 years. Thus, there is almost twice the employment stability at Toyota relative to its U.S. counterparts. Furthermore, a study by Susan Helper and Mari Sako also found greater stability of employment among supplier employees in Japan. In a sample of 472 executives of Japanese suppliers and 671 executives at U.S. suppliers, Helper and Sako found that Japanese sup-plier executives had been with their companies an average of 22 years, while U.S. executives had only been with their companies for 11 years.[33] This stability leads to greater trust within the extended enterprise because suppliers have greater confidence that interorganizational processes will not change and personal ties and interpersonal trust develop between employees in the two organizations.

The previous three practices have been important in helping Toyota build trusting supplier relationships in both the United States and Japan. However, in addition to these practices, Toyota uses two other important practices to build trust with suppliers that are unique to Japan.

Career Paths Between Firms

Toyota also builds trust by requiring career paths in which employees transfer from firm to firm (or are simply allowed to work at partner firm facilities). Employee transfers, both temporary (usually two years) and permanent, are common between Toyota and its suppliers. Thus, job rotations occur across firm boundaries within the extended enter-prise. MIT professor Michael Cusumano has described how executive transfers were particularly important in the auto industry because they "usually preceded technical assistance, loans, or exclusive procurement contracts." It is important to note that Cusumano found that employee transfers *preceded* additional partner-specific investments on the part of the automakers.[34] The point is this: Toyota is more likely to make investments in suppliers when it trusts the individuals it is dealing with—and who better to trust than former employees or people with whom you have worked for years? In my study I found that 23 percent of the top managers at Toyota's affiliated suppliers (suppliers in whom Toyota owns some stock) were former Toyota employees. Almost one-fourth of the top executives at Toyota's partner suppliers are former Toyota employees. Clearly, this is an unusual practice (in the United States) which helps Toyota and its suppliers work cooperatively.

Moreover, in addition to permanent and temporary employee swaps, suppliers often send guest engineers to work at Toyota's technical center on an ongoing basis. I previously discussed how this is an important practice that facilitates information sharing and improves product quality and speed to market. In 1997 Toyota had roughly 700 guest engineers housed at its main technical center in Japan. These engineers are a part of the design team and are given desks in the same room with the Toyota engineers. Thus, supplier and automaker engineers jointly design the component for a new car model. Supplier engineers may work at Toyota's facility for as long as two to three years. Not only do these career-path practices help build trust within the extended enterprise, but also transferred and guest employees are better able to understand how to optimize the efficiency of the extended enterprise because they know both customer and supplier operations.

Minority Ownership

By now its no secret that Japanese firms like Toyota, instead of vertically integrating, will often take significant minority ownership positions in key suppliers. This is an important practice for creating an attitude of mutual destiny and cooperation within the extended enterprise. For example, Toyota owns roughly 28 percent (on average) of the shares of its major supplier partners. This is a significant enough ownership stake to build goal congruence—and trust—between Toyota and its supplier partners. Stock ownership in Japanese trading relationships represent credible commitments that firms have made to each other, and in many ways they are an arrangement that is akin to an "exchange of hostages." If I own a portion of my partner supplier, then I am less willing to take advantage of that supplier because I will be hurt financially. Moreover, I benefit financially when he is successful.

Conclusion

In this chapter I demonstrated that trust creates value in supplier-automaker relationships and is a potential source of collaborative advantage. Trust in supplier-buyer relations is a particularly importance resource in industrial settings where transaction costs are high (e.g., due to environmental uncertainty and a need for investments in dedicated assets) and there is a high value associated with information sharing due to product complexity and industry uncertainty. I argued that transaction costs are significant in the automotive industry and provided evidence that high levels of trust within the extended enterprise can substantially reduce those transaction costs. Indeed, Toyota, the most trusted automaker, had procurement (transaction) costs that were roughly one-fifth those of General Motors, the least trusted automaker. Trust also increased knowledge sharing within the extended enterprise.

Beyond demonstrating that trust creates economic value, I examined how to develop trusting relationships within the extended enterprise. Surprisingly, I found that Toyota's ability to develop trust with suppliers was not based primarily on personal relationships. Nor was it based primarily on stock ownership. Rather, it was based on the fairness and predictability of Toyota's routines and processes for dealing with suppliers (notably selecting suppliers and providing assistance to suppliers). In addition to these processes, employment stability, career paths between firms, and minority stock ownership are practices that help facilitate trust within Toyota's extended enterprise.

In the last three chapters I have described and documented the competitive advantages that Toyota enjoys by creating an extended enterprise characterized by a high degree of trust, knowledge sharing, and dedicated asset investments. Toyota is clearly the industry leader on a large number of measures. But is Toyota simply a unique Japanese firm? Are these ideas replicable within the United States by an American company with a different history, perhaps one with an adversarial history with suppliers? The next three chapters address the process by which firms can create collaborative advantage. They describe the results of a six-year study of Chrysler, a company that has successfully created an extended enterprise, including transforming adversarial arm's-length relationships to cooperative and trusting relationships. From this work emerged a blueprint of steps that other companies might take to build their own extended enterprises.

5

Chrysler's Extended Enterprise: The Process

But if pure *keiretsu* are un-American, the U.S. can still learn from them. By collaborating on research and production, *keiretsu* members regularly deliver new products ahead of lone-wolf rivals ... and at lower costs.... U.S. companies can no longer ignore these advantages.... In short, there's a pressing need for U.S. manufacturers to develop something similar to *keiretsu*.

—*Business Week*

In the spring of 1992, General Motor's purchasing czar, Jose Ignacio Lopez, instructed his troops that cozy supplier relationships were a thing of the past. Every supplier would have to re-win its business in a new round of bidding. A new policy dictated that GM's buyers were not to be wined and dined by suppliers. In fact, buyers were not allowed to accept a lunch invitation except under certain conditions— and even that was discouraged. Furthermore, suppliers were not to be viewed as partners. According to one GM executive: "We don't know what a supplier partnership gets you. It just locks you in. We don't even like using the word *partner*."[1]

Down the road in Auburn Hills, Chrysler's purchasing chief, Thomas Stallkamp, was moving supplier relationships in a markedly different direction. In stark contrast to GM, Stallkamp instructed his buyers to take a supplier to lunch and ask for SCORE (cost reduction) ideas. Stated Chrysler's director of procurement strategy, John Maples: "We wanted suppliers to know we're different. We have to be smarter at leveraging our suppliers' resources and getting more out of suppliers.

We can't pull a Lopez and use brute force."[2] As Stallkamp would later observe, "Lopez unwittingly helped us in our battle for the hearts, minds, and resources of suppliers."[3]

Chrysler's "take a supplier to lunch" tactic was just one in a series of moves designed to transform Chrysler's adversarial supplier relationships to supplier partnerships. Chrysler's new approach was taken out of desperation, in an attempt to compete more effectively with its Japanese competitors, notably Toyota, Honda, and Nissan. Indeed, during the late 1980s and early 1990s, manufacturers in the United States and elsewhere came to the realization that it was virtually impossible to deliver new products to market as quickly and with the same cost and quality as their leading Japanese competitors. Individual manufacturers in the United States were unable to effectively compete because they worked alone while competing against a team of Japanese companies (sometimes called the Japanese *keiretsu*). In response to competition from Japanese companies like Toyota, Honda, Sony, and Matsushita, many U.S. manufacturers have attempted to imitate the production and supplier management methods of Japanese companies. In doing so, they have cut costs in the last decade by overhauling their supplier bases. They have radically pruned the ranks of their suppliers and given more work to the survivors in return for lower prices. And by getting their remaining suppliers to deliver parts just in time and to take responsibility for quality, they have managed to slash inventories, reduce defects, and improve the efficiency of their own production lines.

But these actions have only helped manufacturers survive rather than get ahead. Now manufacturers must wring even greater benefits from their suppliers as they search for more innovative products, faster product development, and lower costs. But as many managers are now beginning to realize, accomplishing the first stage was relatively easy because it did not require altering the nature of their relationship with suppliers. The traditional adversarial relationship remained: Manufacturers continued to design products largely without input from suppliers, to pick suppliers on the basis of price through a competitive bidding process, and to dictate the detailed terms of the contract. They continued to expect suppliers to do as they were told and not much more.

In sharp contrast, the next stage—creating an extended enterprise that involves suppliers in product development and process improvement—requires radically changing the nature of the relationship. It requires a bona fide partnership, in which there is an unimpeded two-way flow of ideas. Although many managers now talk about their desire to turn their suppliers into partners, the fact of the matter is that actually doing it—after decades of exploiting suppliers by pitting one against the other—is exceedingly difficult. Indeed, the task is so difficult that some executives wonder whether Toyota's extended enterprise model can, or even should, be transplanted to the United States, where competitive, contractual, arm's-length relationships between manufacturers and their suppliers have long been the norm. They rightly point out that the partnerships among the members of Toyota's *keiretsu* grew out of cultural and historical experiences that are very different from those that shaped U.S. industries and companies.

However, Chrysler Corporation has shown that it is possible for a U.S. company to make the transition. Chrysler's experience demonstrates not only that a modified form of the *keiretsu* model can work in the United States but also that the benefits can be enormous. Since 1989, Chrysler has shrunk its production supplier base from 2,500 companies to roughly 1,000 and has fundamentally changed the way it works with those that remain. Instead of forcing suppliers to win its business anew every two years, Chrysler now gives most of them business for the life of a model and beyond; excruciatingly detailed contracts have given way to oral agreements. Instead of relying solely on its own engineers to create the concept for a new car and then to design all the car's components, Chrysler now involves suppliers. And instead of Chrysler dictating prices to suppliers, regardless of whether the prices are realistic or fair, the two sides now strive together to find ways to lower the costs of making cars and to share the savings.

The results have been astounding. The time Chrysler needs to develop a new vehicle is approaching 160 weeks, down from an average of 234 weeks during the 1980s. The cost of developing a new vehicle has plunged an estimated 20–40 percent during the last decade. And, at the same time, Chrysler has managed to produce one consumer hit after another. As a result, Chrysler's profit per vehicle has jumped from an average of $250 in the 1980s to a record (for all U.S. automakers) of $2,110 in 1996.

Of course, Chrysler's astounding comeback is hardly news anymore. But one crucial aspect of the story deserves greater attention: exactly how the company managed to transform its contentious relationships with its suppliers. Believing that Chrysler's turnaround might hold lessons for other U.S. manufacturers, I undertook a six-year study of the company's revival. From 1992 to 1998, I interviewed and surveyed dozens of Chrysler executives and managers as well as 33 of the company's largest first-tier suppliers. I also analyzed thousands of pages of Chrysler's internal documents.

From this work emerged a blueprint of the steps that other companies might take to build an extended enterprise, or what we might think of as an American-style *keiretsu*. By benchmarking competitors, listening to suppliers, and experimenting with ideas and programs, Chrysler's top management team of Robert Lutz, president; Thomas Stallkamp, head of purchasing; François Castaing, head of vehicle engineering; and Glenn Gardner, LH program manager, gradually developed a vision of the changes that Chrysler needed to make. They came to realize that people—both at Chrysler and in suppliers' organizations—needed to have a common vision of how to collaborate to create value jointly. They came to recognize that trust in relationships will take root only if both parties share in the rewards and not just the risks. And ultimately they incorporated those realizations into the fabric of the company's management systems.

The steps that Chrysler took were not always by design. But through trial and error, the automaker has managed to develop an extended enterprise that is becoming a model of cooperation and efficiency. In this chapter I explore the process that Chrysler went through to transform its previously adversarial supplier relationships into cooperative and trusting relationships within its extended enterprise.

The Impetus for Change

In the mid-1980s, as part of an effort to improve its competitiveness, Chrysler conducted an extensive benchmarking study of product development and manufacturing at Honda Motor Company, which was then expanding its manufacturing and sales presence in the United States faster than either Toyota Motor Corporation or Nissan Motor Company. One factor that Chrysler studied was supplier relations.

Honda was organized into product-development teams composed of individuals from all key functions, all of whom had cradle-to-grave responsibility for the development of a vehicle. The teams included suppliers' engineers, who had responsibility for both the design and manufacture of a particular component or system. Executives from Chrysler thought initially that Honda's practices were interesting but completely foreign to Chrysler, which was organized by function and which developed products in a traditional sequential process that did not routinely involve suppliers. Chrysler's engineers designed components and suppliers built them. Whereas Honda selected suppliers that had a history of good relations with the company and a track record for delivering quality products and meeting cost targets, Chrysler selected suppliers that could build components at the lowest possible cost. (Buyers had to obtain quotations from at least three suppliers.) A supplier's track record for performance and quality was relatively unimportant. As a consequence, the typical relationship between Chrysler and its suppliers was characterized by mutual distrust and suspicion. According to purchasing chief Thomas Stallkamp:

> Like other automakers, Chrysler had a long-standing love-hate relationship with suppliers. Every year, we offered new contracts for parts and components, and, naturally, the lowest bidder always won. But something funny happened between the time the bid was awarded and the opening of contracts the following year: The automaker usually became upset with the quality of the parts and materials being shipped, and the supplier often complained about the puny size of the margins. Not surprisingly, confidentiality and trust didn't exist in this system.[4]

Honda's approach suddenly looked less foreign after Chrysler acquired the American Motors Corporation in 1987 for its profitable Jeep operations. AMC had implemented some Honda-like supplier-management and development practices. The reason was necessity.

Because AMC had neither the resources to design all its own parts nor the power of larger automakers to dictate the prices it was willing to pay for them, it had learned to rely on suppliers to engineer and design a number of its vehicles' components. Also, the engineering and manufacturing staff in AMC's Jeep and truck group had been operating for several years as an integrated team. With just 1,000 engineering employees, AMC had developed three vehicles between 1980 and 1987—the Cherokee, the Premier, and the Comanche—and was beginning a fourth, the Allure coupe. In comparison, Chrysler's 5,500 engineers and technicians had developed only four all-new vehicles during the 1980s: the K-car, the minivan, the Dakota truck, and the Shadow/Sundance.

AMC's operations suggested to Chrysler's executives that Japanese-style partnerships might be possible in an American context. Equally important, that discovery occurred at a time when Chrysler's leaders had been made keenly aware that their development process was inadequate. The company's newly launched LH program (Chrysler Concord, Eagle Vision, and Dodge Intrepid—Chrysler's response to Ford's popular Taurus) was running a projected $1 billion over budget, and the company was in dire financial straits. It had a $4.5 billion unfunded pension fund. Its losses were deepening. After closing three plants in 18 months during 1988 and 1989, Chrysler hit rock bottom, reporting a record loss of $664 million in the fourth quarter of 1989. With the exception of the minivan, its boxy cars appealed only to older buyers. As one Chrysler executive observed: "The average age of our car buyers was 59 years. To keep selling cars, we'd have to follow these folks to the graveyard."[5] Chrysler's executives knew they had to do something fast.

Some changes in top management helped. Lutz, who had become president of operations in 1988, championed the effort to adapt and apply the positive lessons learned from Honda and AMC. When Chrysler's chief engineer retired in 1988, Lutz replaced him with François Castaing, AMC's chief engineer. In one of his first moves, Castaing recommended that Chrysler slam the brakes on the LH program, and the company picked Glenn Gardner to rethink and relaunch the program. Gardner had been chairman of Diamond-Star Motors Corporation, Chrysler's joint venture with Mitsubishi Motors Corporation, and was familiar with Mitsubishi's product-development process, which was similar to Honda's.

Lutz, Castaing, and Gardner picked the team to develop the LH, a model code that many at Chrysler darkly joked stood for "last hope." The reborn LH program was to serve as a pilot for redesigning Chrysler's product-development process and supplier relations. To spur creativity and increase the speed of the product-development cycle, the executives made three important changes that broke with tradition. First, to shield the team from internal bureaucracy, they decided to move it away from Highland Park, Michigan, where most of Chrysler's operations were located. Second, to speed decisions internally and to eliminate sequential decision making, they included on the team individuals from design, engineering, manufacturing, procurement, marketing, and finance. Finally, they decided to experiment with new methods of working with suppliers, drawing on the lessons learned from Honda, AMC, and Mitsubishi.

By 1991, Chrysler's senior managers knew they were onto something. The LH was being developed in record time and below the aggressive cost targets set at the beginning of the program. The new approach to product development and working with suppliers was extended to the rest of the company that year.

Chrysler's New Model

Chrysler's new model reflects several important changes in the company's processes for selecting, working with, and evaluating suppliers (see Table 5.1). These changes in the processes of working with suppliers *preceded* changes in the relationship with suppliers (see Table 5.2). Together, these changes have been effective at building trust with suppliers, including getting suppliers to identify with Chrysler's extended enterprise, creating processes and incentives to increase knowledge sharing within the extended enterprise, and increasing the level of dedicated assets within the extended enterprise.

Table 5.1. Chrysler's Partner Strategy *Process* Characteristics

	Arm's-Length Approach	Partner Approach
Supplier selection	Competitive bid • low price wins • selection after design	Pre-source suppliers • Target cost sets price • Selection before design (capability based)
Accountability	Split accountability for design, prototype, testing, and production	Single supplier for design, prototype, testing, and production
Dedicated Asset Investments (e.g., coordination mechanisms)	Minimal investments	Substantial investments (e.g., guest engineers, plants, etc.)
Information Sharing	Discrete activity focus • No formal processes for supplier input	Total value chain focus • Formal process for supplier input
Performance Evaluation	Simple • Unit price	Complex, multifaceted • "Soft" evaluation
Governance/Contracts	Short term	Long term

Table 5.2. Chrysler's Partner Strategy *Relationship* Characteristics

	Arm's-Length Approach	Partner Approach
Relationship Focus	Transaction orientation • No credit for past performance	Relationship orientation • Recognize past performance
Responsibility	No responsibility for supplier profit margins	Recognize supplier needs to make a fair profit
Communication	Directive, one-way communication	Collaborative, two-way communication
Relationship Expectations	No guarantee of business beyond contract	Expectation of relationship beyond contract
Performance Expectations	Explicit in contract	Considerable expectations beyond contract
Relationship/ Work Attitudes	Adversarial • Zero-sum game	Cooperative • Positive-sum game

Building Trust

Co-located Cross-Functional Teams

Chrysler reorganized into five cross-functional vehicle-development teams—one for large cars, one for small cars, one for minivans, one for Jeeps, and one for trucks. I found that Chrysler's new organizational design (the cross-functional team as a permanent organization unit) created the conditions necessary to effectively develop both interorganizational (process-based) trust and interpersonal (relationship-based) trust with suppliers.

Chrysler's reorganization into cross-functional teams was a critical first step in getting its functions to present "one face" to suppliers and to end the conflicting demands and shifting priorities that had characterized its sequential product-development process. As one supplier executive observed: "Before Chrysler reorganized, we were always being whipsawed in different directions. Each function wanted something different and we always had conflicting demands."[6] Cross-functional teams were the starting point for improving continuity, coordination, and trust both within Chrysler and between Chrysler and its suppliers. Suppliers were able to develop more stable relationships with Chrysler's staff and could count on the company to follow through more effectively on promises and agreements. Stated another supplier executive: "[Before the reorganization] people at Chrysler didn't agree with or trust each other, much less us. Their internal coordination was poor and the personnel on a vehicle project were constantly changing. It was difficult to develop stable relationships."[7] By creating a stable organizational unit charged with repeatedly interacting with the same set of suppliers, Chrysler was able to minimize internal communication errors and create a stronger set of internal norms, customs, and priorities. This made Chrysler's behavior more understandable and predictable to the supplier. In turn, this created conditions for trust to develop across organizational boundaries.

To further improve internal coordination, Chrysler built a new facility that allowed for the co-location of platform team members. To illustrate, before Chrysler's Technology Center (CTC) was completed in 1991, Chrysler's small car platform team, which developed the Neon, was located in 14 different buildings around the Detroit area. Face-to-face meetings were very difficult to organize. As one Chrysler executive noted, "it would take days or weeks to set up a meeting; and then you'd have to trudge through the slush and snow from building to building to get together." However, the Chrysler Technology Center, with its 4 million square feet (the size of seven Rose Bowls), allowed for the co-location of all Neon team members on the fourth floor. It also had room for the co-location of more than 300 supplier engineers. According to the Neon procurement manager: "It made a definite difference being here. It absolutely improved communication.... Proximity is very important for people sharing ideas and learning from each other. It's easy to communicate and coordinate vehicle development activities internally and with suppliers."[8] Thus, interestingly enough, Chrysler's ability to improve coordination and trust with suppliers was, to a large degree, dependent on its ability to improve coordination and trust internally. As one supplier executive observed; "Chrysler was finally on the same page. Everyone in the Chrysler organization, from Bob Lutz down to the release engineer, was consistent in their message to suppliers."[9]

Pre-sourcing and Target Costing

The next step Chrysler took to build supplier trust was to eliminate competitive bidding in favor of pre-sourcing. *Pre-sourcing* means choosing suppliers early in the vehicle's concept-development stage and giving them significant, if not total, responsibility for designing a given component or system. The rationale for pre-sourcing is that it permits many engineering tasks to be carried out simultaneously rather than sequentially, thereby speeding up the development process.

In addition to having responsibility for design, most pre-sourced suppliers are responsible for building prototypes during development and for manufacturing the component or system in volume once the vehicle is in commercial production. This new practice means that suppliers of such complex components as the heating and air-conditioning system join the product development effort very early and, as prime contractors, take total responsibility for the cost, quality, and on-time delivery of their systems. Suppliers say this approach gives them more flexibility in developing effective solutions to problems.

In the past, Chrysler had often given responsibility for design, manufacture of prototypes, and volume production of a component to separate companies, resulting in a lack of accountability. When suppliers had problems producing a component at the required cost or quality, they would often blame their troubles on the design—not surprising, given that some studies have found that 70 percent of quality problems in automotive components are due to poor design.[10] Consequently, Chrysler and its suppliers would waste time trying to assign blame for problems when they could have been trying to solve them.

To overcome that fragmented approach, Chrysler had to dispense with competitive bidding. For the LH project, Chrysler's corporate purchasing department gave the project's cross-functional platform team a pre-qualified list of suppliers considered to have the most advanced engineering and manufacturing capabilities. That team, which included people from engineering, quality control, and purchasing, then selected suppliers on the basis of proven ability to design and manufacture the component or system.

The new process also required Chrysler to decide how to set a fair price for the component. Under the old bidding process, the price of a component or system was deemed fair because it was market driven. However, under the new system, Chrysler had to choose the supplier before the component was even designed. Chrysler decided to adopt the widely used Japanese practice of *target costing*, which involves determining what price the market, or end customer, will pay for the vehicle and then working backward to calculate the allowable costs for systems, subsystems, and components.

How did the company set the initial target costs in the LH program? "Actually, we set them somewhat unscientifically and then, when necessary, had the suppliers convince us that another number was better," says Barry Price, Chrysler's executive director of platform supply for procurement and supply. "We would involve suppliers and tell them, 'I've got X amount of money.' We would let them know what functions the part or system in question would be required to perform and ask, 'Can you supply it for that cost?' Usually, their response would be no, but they at least came back with some alternatives. The first time through, we had to find our way. The second time, we had the benefit of history and, as a result, we developed better targets at the outset of the program."[11]

Target costing has shifted Chrysler's relationship with suppliers from a zero-sum game to a positive-sum game. Historically, Chrysler put constant pressure on suppliers to reduce prices, regardless of whether the suppliers had reduced their costs; the automaker did not feel responsible for the suppliers' profit margin. Chrysler's new focus on cost instead of price has created a win-win situation with suppliers because the company works *with* suppliers to meet common cost and functional objectives. This philosophy is critical if trusting partnerships are to take root in the extended enterprise.

Long-Term Commitments

Finally, to earn its suppliers' trust and to encourage them to invest in dedicated assets, Chrysler gives its suppliers long-term commitments. The average length of the contracts held by a sample of 48 of Chrysler's suppliers on the LH program in 1994 was 4.4 years. By comparison, Chrysler's supply contracts lasted 2.1 years on average in 1989, according to a 1991 study by Susan Helper.[12]

Today Chrysler has given oral guarantees to more than 90 percent of its suppliers that they will have the business for the life of the model they are supplying and beyond. Of course, the suppliers must fulfill one condition: They must perform well on the current model and must meet the target cost on the next. "The business is theirs to keep forever or until they elect to lose it," Stallkamp declares. He cites the fact that Chrysler only replaced 11 suppliers out of roughly 300 on the last LH program (Chrysler Concorde, Eagle Vision, Dodge Intrepid) as evidence that they have demonstrated their commitment to suppliers.

Suppliers make it clear that Chrysler's long-term commitments are having the desired effect. "I would certainly say that we are more comfortable making investments and taking risks on behalf of Chrysler than our other U.S. customers. We simply have a more secure long-term future,"[13] says the CEO of one Chrysler supplier.

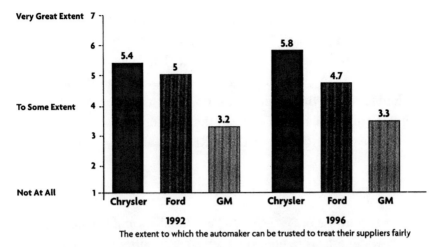

Figure 5.1. Evidence That Chrysler Has Increased Supplier Trust

Surveys I conducted in 1992 and 1996 confirm that Chrysler has made tremendous strides in developing cooperative, trusting relationships with its suppliers relative to Ford and GM. In 1992, suppliers rated Chrysler as slightly more trustworthy than Ford and quite a bit more trustworthy than GM. By 1996, Chrysler had increased the spread and was rated significantly more trustworthy than both Ford and GM. Interestingly, Chrysler was not always the most trusted automaker. In fact, in a supplier survey that Chrysler had done in 1990, Chrysler was rated as the *least* trustworthy automaker. Thus, in just 6 years, Chrysler transformed itself from the least, to the most, trusted U.S. automaker (See Figure 5.1).

Enterprise-Wide Knowledge Sharing: The SCORE Program

The next step in building supplier partnerships is to figure out how to motivate them to participate in continuous improvement processes for the value chain as a whole. Eliciting the full effort and total resources of suppliers is critical because partnerships are effective only when both parties work to expand the pie. Such cooperation is possible only when the supplier trusts the buyer and when the two parties *really* communicate.

Chrysler began to build trust and improve communications with a small set of suppliers during the pilot LH vehicle program. However, it was another program, one that Chrysler began to develop in 1990, that became, almost by accident, the company's most important method for improving communication, lowering costs, and ultimately building trust. The formal name of that program now is the Supplier Cost Reduction Effort (dubbed SCORE).

Asking for Help

The basic purpose of SCORE is to help suppliers and Chrysler reduce system-wide costs without hurting suppliers' profits. The catalyst for the SCORE program was a speech that president Robert Lutz gave at the Detroit Athletic Club in August 1989 to executives from 25 of Chrysler's largest suppliers. Lutz told the suppliers that because of Chrysler's desperate situation, he wanted their assistance and ideas on how the company could lower both its own costs and those of its suppliers. The message was, "All I want is your brainpower, not your margins."

The fledgling efforts in the LH program to build tighter relationships with suppliers were bearing fruit, and Chrysler's leaders were eager to maintain the momentum. At the time, General Motors was putting the squeeze on suppliers, demanding across-the-board price cuts. In his speech, Lutz stressed that Chrysler wanted to take a different path.

After his speech, the suppliers crowded around Lutz eager to offer their ideas. Lutz was so impressed by many of the ideas that he decided to initiate a formal process for reviewing, approving, and implementing them. Given Chrysler's history of adversarial relationships with suppliers, one might ask why they did not react cynically to Lutz's request for help. For one, they knew that Chrysler was on the ropes. In addition, Chrysler had four relatively new leaders who had demonstrated a commitment to radical change: Lutz, Castaing, Gardner, and Stallkamp, the purchasing chief who, in early 1990, had replaced a champion of competitive bidding. There was also some hard evidence of Chrysler's sincerity: the relaunched LH program.

Lutz kept the ball rolling after the speech. He was so impressed with the suppliers' ideas and willingness to share information that he had senior executives schedule follow-up meetings with them. To get advice on how Chrysler could accomplish that task more systematically, a small group of senior executives, including Castaing and Stallkamp, visited a number of key suppliers. These unusual visits impressed the suppliers, many of whom were upset with GM's heavy-handed treatment.

During these talks, many suppliers complained about how GM was demanding across-the-board price cuts—a move that would require them to lower their costs—when, from their perspective, GM could not even get its own house in order. The suppliers noted that Chrysler, too, was far from perfect. Indeed, Chrysler had long been guilty of turning down or simply ignoring potentially money-saving suggestions from its suppliers—for instance, recommendations that they use a different material in a component—because the suggestions would have required running tests and making other changes in the component or in Chrysler's processes. In many cases, engineers refused even to consider such proposals because considering them would have increased their workloads. Others were overly fearful of taking risks.

Unveiling SCORE

It was based on these discussions with suppliers that Chrysler established SCORE as a formal program that committed the automaker to encouraging, reviewing, and acting on suppliers' ideas quickly and fairly, and to sharing the benefits of those ideas with the suppliers. The SCORE program was unveiled in 1990 at a meeting with Chrysler's top 150 suppliers. To emphasize its desire to change, Chrysler specifically asked suppliers to suggest operational changes that it could make in its own organization to reduce both its costs and those of the suppliers. Chrysler soon received a large number of written suggestions.

Chrysler's executives knew that the initiative would fail if the company rejected all the ideas or did not respond quickly. So in another display of strong leadership, Chrysler's top managers took personal responsibility for making sure that the company followed through on its promise to review and act on the proposals quickly.

Castaing, Stallkamp, and other senior executives met each month to review the proposals and evaluate Chrysler's responses. Initially, Chrysler's engineers wanted to reject many ideas, and senior managers had to decide when to overrule them. Determined to avoid a not-invented-here reaction, Castaing forced through some of the ideas, pacifying the engineers by telling them to give the ideas a try simply as an experiment. Enough of the early ideas were accepted to convince suppliers that Chrysler really was open to suggestions. Soon new suggestions were pouring in, and the successes helped break down the engineers' resistance.

To get suppliers to buy into the SCORE program, Chrysler took three steps. First, it focused on what Chrysler itself was doing wrong. Second, it asked suppliers to make suggestions for changes that involved materials or parts provided by lower-tier suppliers. Only as a third step did it turn to what the key suppliers—the ones that made strategic components or systems—were doing wrong. "The order with which we addressed these issues was important," Chrysler's Barry Price says. "The suppliers never would have gone for self-criticism before we developed a track record of correcting our own problems."[14]

Why were suppliers willing to take the risk of expending resources to offer such ideas? The answer is that Chrysler made it profitable for them to participate in SCORE and demonstrated that it would play fair. "For many, when we fixed our operations, they made huge savings," Price says. Perhaps even more important, Chrysler offered to share the savings generated by the suppliers' suggestions with the suppliers. Partly because it did not have the resources to audit suppliers and partly to promote trust, Chrysler initially did not quibble when it suspected that a supplier was grabbing more than half. "That first time we found out a supplier wasn't being fair with us, we didn't ask for a renegotiation," recalls Price. "We just let them know that we knew. The result: We began to get more and more ideas—sometimes even on products they didn't supply."[15] In one case, a supplier suggested that Chrysler stop making a part out of magnesium and use plastic—an improvement that would cost the supplier the business. That suggestion saved Chrysler more than $100,000 per year.

Beyond the incentive of improving their own profitability and increasing their business with Chrysler, suppliers appreciated being listened to for a change. Under the traditional system, suppliers were rarely asked for their ideas or suggestions for improvement; they were simply given a discrete task and asked to perform that task for a price.

Incorporating SCORE

In 1992, Chrysler made SCORE a formal part of its supplier rating system. Chrysler began to reward those suppliers that offered ideas for improvement and that made efforts to improve the Chrysler extended enterprise. Today, Chrysler keeps detailed records of the number of proposals each supplier makes and the dollar savings they generate. Chrysler uses those figures—along with the supplier's performance in the areas of price, quality, delivery, and technology—to grade the supplier's overall performance. A supplier's SCORE rating represents 15 percent of its overall performance rating, up from 8 percent in 1994—an indication of how much Chrysler values continuous improvement throughout its value chain.

Since February 1994, Chrysler has given suppliers specific annual targets for savings from SCORE ideas. Although Chrysler does not penalize a supplier if it misses a SCORE target, the supplier's performance over time may eventually determine how much business it receives from the automaker. Suppliers are expected to offer suggestions that result in cost reductions equaling 5 percent of the supplier's sales to Chrysler. The automaker also has expanded the program to enlist suppliers' assistance in reducing vehicle weight, warranty claims, and complexity. (For example, suppliers receive a $20,000 credit for every part removed from a system.)

Chrysler also tracks the number of proposals awaiting a decision and the amount of time it takes to respond to a proposal. Although the job no longer falls to senior executives, Chrysler's managers continue to review engineers' evaluations of supplier suggestions. Managers also help suppliers with the SCORE paperwork and routinely intercede on the suppliers' behalf. In other words, the managers serve as the suppliers' advocates within the company. And to make submitting ideas even easier, SCORE is now an online process: A supplier can submit a proposal or check on its status at any time.

When Chrysler accepts a SCORE idea, the supplier has two choices: It can claim its half of the savings or it can share more of the savings with Chrysler in order to boost its performance rating and potentially obtain more business. To understand more clearly how SCORE works, consider the experience of Magna International, one of Chrysler's largest suppliers. Magna provides Chrysler with seat systems, interior door and trim panels, engine and transmission systems, and a wide variety of other products. In 1993, Magna made its initial SCORE proposal, suggesting that Chrysler use a different woodgrain material on a decorative exterior molding on its minivan. The material Magna recommended cost less and offered the same quality as the material they had been using. After receiving the proposal, the Chrysler buyer notified engineering and requested its review and consent. The entire process took approximately two weeks. Chrysler approved the proposal, which resulted in annual savings of $250,000. Between 1992 and 1996, Magna submitted 213 additional SCORE proposals, 129 of which Chrysler approved—for a total cost savings of $75.5 million. Rather than grab a share of these savings, Magna has opted to give 100 percent of them to Chrysler in the hopes of boosting its performance rating and winning more business. The result: From 1990 to 1996, Magna's sales to Chrysler have more than doubled, from $635 million to $1.45 billion. What is more, the greater economies of scale mean that the business with Chrysler is now more profitable, says John Brice, the Magna executive director in charge of the Chrysler account.

SCORE has been astoundingly successful. In its first two years of operation, 1990 and 1991, it generated 875 ideas worth $170.8 million in annual savings to Chrysler. In 1994, suppliers submitted 3,786 ideas, which produced $504 million in annual savings. In 1998 SCORE generated more than $2 billion in savings to Chrysler, almost 25 percent of Chrysler's record profits.

Beyond the SCORE program, Chrysler has taken a number of other steps to facilitate interaction and knowledge sharing with suppliers. For example, Chrysler was early in developing a common email system, and it has also established an advisory board of executives from its top 14 suppliers. In addition, it has instituted an annual meeting of

its top 150 strategic suppliers and holds quarterly meetings with each individually to discuss strategic and performance issues and to review priorities for the coming year.

Dedicated Assets

Suppliers have demonstrated their trust in Chrysler by increasing their investments in dedicated assets—plants, equipment, systems, processes, and people dedicated exclusively to serving Chrysler's needs. To coordinate communication with and across suppliers more effectively, Chrysler has imitated the Japanese practice of employing *resident engineers*—suppliers' engineers who work side by side with Chrysler's employees. The number of resident engineers in Chrysler's facilities has soared from fewer than 30 in 1989 to more than 900 today. Executives at suppliers and at Chrysler claim that this practice has resulted in greater trust and more reliable and timely communication of important information. In addition to the resident engineers, nearly all suppliers have purchased CATIA (Chrysler's preferred Computer Aided Design/Computer Aided Manufacturing software), which at $40,000 per engineer is no small investment. (To help them obtain a lower price for CATIA, Chrysler arranged a large-scale group purchase for more than 250 suppliers within its extended enterprise.)

A number of suppliers also have invested in dedicated facilities to improve their ability to make just-in-time deliveries to Chrysler and to provide it with better service. For example, Textron built a plant dedicated to producing interior trim parts for the LH and located a new design facility less than two miles from the Chrysler Technology Center. Dana recently built a $14 million plant in Brazil that is dedicated to producing a rolling chassis exclusively for Chrysler. Partly as a result of such investments, the average distance between Chrysler's assembly plants and its suppliers' facilities has been decreasing. At Chrysler's plant in Belvidere, Illinois, where the Neon is assembled, the number of supplier shipment points has dropped by 43 percent, and the average distance from supplier to assembler plant has shrunk by 26 miles. This geographic proximity, as I showed in chapter 2, lowers inventory costs and enhances communication.

Chrysler's Extended Enterprise: An American *Keiretsu*

The extended enterprise that Chrysler has created differs from Toyota's *keiretsu* in three major respects. First, Toyota owns 20–50 percent of the equity of its largest suppliers; Chrysler does not and could not take similar stakes. Toyota, for example, has only about 310 suppliers, and those with which it has equity ties, about 30, typically depend on it for two-thirds of their sales. So their destinies are closely intertwined. By comparison, Chrysler still has a much larger group of suppliers, and few of its most important suppliers depend on it for a majority of their sales. Second, approximately 20 percent of the executives at Toyota's major supplier companies formerly worked for Toyota. This intimacy leads to a high level of understanding and a common culture that Chrysler could never duplicate. Third, Chrysler's extended enterprise is still well behind Toyota's in its ability to facilitate knowledge sharing among suppliers. Chrysler does not have a supplier association nor does it have *jishuken* groups. And it has only recently begun providing direct consulting help to suppliers, but on a much smaller scale than Toyota.

However, Chrysler's arrangement has its advantages. First, it is much easier for Chrysler to drop underperforming suppliers than it is for Toyota. Because Toyota cannot drop suppliers very easily, it is under greater pressure to commit resources to help suppliers improve. This assistance almost certainly benefits rivals—including Chrysler—that buy from those suppliers (for example, Denso, Toyota's largest supplier, has become a major partner supplier to Chrysler).

Second, Chrysler's formal programs (i.e., SCORE) that measure results and offer incentives for information sharing and improvement ideas are probably more suitable for the U.S. business environment than Toyota's relatively informal approach would be. One could argue that without formal programs such as SCORE, suppliers would not devote the same resources to generating ideas. As Stallkamp observed: "SCORE is a success because it is a communications program, not just a cost-cutting program. By learning how to communicate, we've learned how to help each other."[16] The level of communication needed

to make a supplier partnership productive simply may not happen naturally in the U.S. business environment.

On the other hand, Chrysler's policies for building partnerships seem to be too successful in one sense: They appear to be making it harder for the company to continue to shrink its supplier base, which it would like to do to reduce coordination costs, improve quality, achieve even greater economies of scale, and, last but not least, strengthen its ties with the suppliers it retains. The shrinkage rate has slowed. Chrysler still has almost four times as many suppliers in the United States as Toyota does in Japan.

In addition, Chrysler still lags far behind Toyota in converting lower levels of its supply chain to the new supplier-management approach. Its biggest suppliers are only beginning to replicate programs such as pre-sourcing, target costing, and SCORE in their own supply chains. In contrast, the majority of Toyota's first-tier suppliers in Japan have their own supplier associations and other programs to help develop their suppliers (I will discuss this in greater detail in chapter 8). Thus, successful ideas spread much more quickly throughout the entire supply chain within Toyota's extended enterprise. But Chrysler's extended enterprise is clearly catching up.

Conclusion

Although Chrysler has a long way to go, the progress it has made since 1990 is remarkable. Its success to date in building the Chrysler Extended Enterprise—a term Chrysler's leaders have coined (and trademarked) to refer to its new philosophy of working with suppliers—proves that decades of adversarial supplier relations can be overcome. By creating a stable organization unit to work with suppliers (the platform team), eliminating competitive bidding, and giving long-term commitments, Chrysler has dramatically increased supplier trust. As supplier trust increased, Chrysler was able to implement knowledge-sharing programs such as SCORE, and suppliers were increasingly willing to invest in people, processes, and facilities that were dedicated to Chrysler. The result is a production network that works as a team like never before—a team that works in ways similar to Toyota's vertical *keiretsu* in Japan. As Steve Zimmer, Chrysler's director of operations and strategy for procurement and supply, noted, "We've learned that you don't have to be Japanese to have a *keiretsu*-like relationship with suppliers."[17] Chrysler has decisively shown that highly productive partnerships with suppliers can flourish in the United States.

6

Chrysler's Extended Enterprise: The Results

Chrysler's profit performance in 1993 was simply staggering. The profit per
unit it achieved is the highest in the history of the Industry Report Card.

—*Automotive Industries*

The quotation above from *Automotive Industries* reveals that Chrysler's
profit performance, beginning in 1993, hit levels never before seen in the
U.S. automobile industry (at least in the last 25 years since *Automotive
Industries* began tracking profitability). And 1993 was no fluke. In fact,
Chrysler surpassed its 1993 profit per unit performance to achieve
record profits in 1994, 1996, and 1997 (1995 did not exceed 1993 but it
was still more than 100 percent higher than what Chrysler had achieved
in any year in the 1980s). Chrysler's "staggering" level of performance
has been possible due to the advantages of the extended enterprise
model. According to Chrysler executives, Chrysler has dramatically
improved its performance since 1989 primarily due to the platform
team structure and the extended enterprise or partner model of supplier relationships. Stated purchasing chief Thomas Stallkamp, "Those
of us who lived through [the turnaround] know that working with suppliers is how we were able to change the company.[1] Stallkamp and others claim that these changes have resulted in measurable improvements
in the speed of product development, new vehicle development costs,
and procurement (transaction) costs. In turn, they insist that these
improvements have increased Chrysler's marketshare and profitabil-

ity. Undoubtedly, other factors have also contributed to Chrysler's success. For example, Chrysler's cars have been recognized for their distinctive styling (in particular, "cab forward" design). However, the fact that SCORE (Chrysler's cost reduction program with suppliers) alone accounted for roughly 20 percent of Chrysler's record 1996 pretax profits is strong evidence that partnering has been a *major* contributor to Chrysler's success. Chrysler has further affirmed its belief in the value of partnerships by promoting procurement chief Thomas Stallkamp to the Chrysler presidency, the first time in 25 years (and perhaps ever) that a procurement head has been promoted to this position.

My research on Chrysler shows that the extended enterprise model has helped Chrysler achieve amazing results in a number of key areas that are highly correlated with profitability. By establishing an extended enterprise (implementing the changes described in the previous chapter) Chrysler has been able to speed product development, lower product development costs, lower production costs, lower transaction costs, and improve quality. In addition, the partnership model results in benefits that are not easily quantifiable, such as higher employee morale and greater work satisfaction associated with cooperative supplier-buyer work relationships. In the remainder of this chapter, I examine how and why Chrysler has been able to realize substantial performance improvement in each of the areas listed above.

Speed-to-Market Economies

Perhaps the most important benefit of the extended enterprise is speed—the ability to respond quickly to market opportunities. Company documents indicate that Chrysler has reduced the amount of time it takes to develop a new vehicle by almost 40 percent, from 234 weeks to 160 weeks (see Figure 6.1). As a result, Chrysler has developed twice as many all-new vehicles in the 1990s as the 1980s. Further, according to *Automotive News,* Chrysler's current product-development cycle time is 28 months compared to Ford's at 36 months.[2] GM does not share information on its lead times, but GM is widely recognized in the industry as having the slowest product-development cycle times among the Big Three.

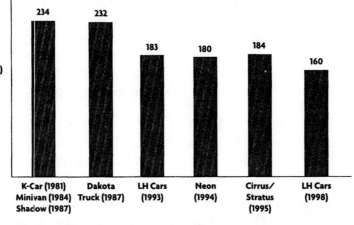

Figure 6.1. Chrysler's Extended Enterprise Speeds Product Development

(*Source:* Chrysler Corporation, Procurement & Supply)

The partner model economizes on time spent in product development in four ways. First, partnering minimizes the time spent searching for suppliers as well as the time spent negotiating contracts and bargaining over prices. Under the competitive bidding system, roughly 12–18 months of the development process were devoted to sending out bids for quotes, analyzing bids, rebidding, negotiating contracts, and "bringing the suppliers up to speed." Chrysler and its suppliers spent significant time on contract negotiations due to mistrust and the belief that the profits generated in the exchange relationship would not be shared fairly. However, today Chrysler and its suppliers devote less time to contract negotiation and price bargaining because suppliers are confident that the gains will be split fairly. As one Chrysler buyer noted: "We used to spend lots of time on the bidding process and working through the details of the contract. Today, we may not even worry about signing a contract."[3]

A second way that the partner model speeds product development is by minimizing the time delays that result from a sequential development process. States Glenn Gardner, the program manager on the LH pilot program:

> We had a lengthy, sequential, "throw it over the wall" approach to the way we designed and built a new vehicle. After the design

studio had the car styled, engineering would begin work and find many things not feasible that would require redesign. Then, after the engineering job was completed, we "threw it over the wall" to purchasing. Again, there would be more redesign because suppliers—involved too late in the process—either could not make the part, or else could not make it economically.[4]

Without a supplier partnership, the speed advantages of simultaneous engineering are impossible because the development effort at the supplier cannot begin until the automaker has completed the design. The automaker simply cannot begin working with the supplier at the beginning of the product-development process because it must first design the part in order to use competitive bidding to select the supplier. As a result, there are considerably more design changes—and more changes close to volume production—with the traditional approach compared to the extended enterprise. This is well illustrated by the data given to me by a supplier who tracked the number of engineering changes, and the timing of those changes, for two vehicle development projects—one where the automaker used an arm's-length approach to supplier management and the other where the automaker used a partnership approach to working with suppliers. The data (presented in Figure 6.2) show that using the partnership model the supplier experienced more engineering changes early in the product-development cycle but fewer changes late in the product-development cycle. Overall, there were many more engineering changes late in the product-development process that created delays with the automaker employing the arm's-length process. As one supplier executive noted: "We have many more engineering changes when the automaker uses a sequential product development process. Naturally that slows down time to market. It's simply unavoidable."[5]

A third reason that the partnering model speeds the product-development cycle is that it gives suppliers additional time to search for solutions to design or production problems. Under Chrysler's competitive bidding regime, the supplier typically did not know it had won the business until approximately 75–100 weeks before volume production or "Job 1." Under the new system, suppliers are selected and involved at the product concept stage, which historically has been

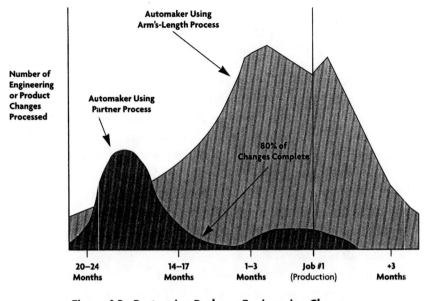

Number of Engineering or Product Changes Processed

Automaker Using Arm's-Length Process

Automaker Using Partner Process

80% of Changes Complete

| 20–24 Months | 14–17 Months | 1–3 Months | Job #1 (Production) | +3 Months |

Figure 6.2. Partnering Reduces Engineering Changes

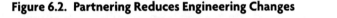

Note: For confidentiality reasons, actual data on number of engineering changes is not reported.

roughly 180 weeks before volume production. Thus, suppliers have an extra 18–24 months to prepare for volume production. Stated Neon procurement manager Bernie Bedard:

> Sourcing [on the Neon] began 200 weeks before volume production. All major systems and components were sourced by 150 weeks. We felt we needed to give suppliers the earliest opportunity possible to meet the aggressive targets ... we recognized their needs in terms of technology, training, capital, etc. We responded to suppliers who told us, "If you come to me with a request one year before action is needed, I am limited in comparison to my options if you come two years earlier."[6]

Finally, supplier investments in dedicated assets, notably Chrysler-specific coordination mechanisms (e.g., resident engineers, dedicated design facilities, EDI, Catia) have resulted in more timely and efficient communication, thereby speeding the flow and accuracy of information between Chrysler and its suppliers. Thus, investments in coordination mechanisms within the extended enterprise have also helped to reduce the length of the product-development cycle. This includes Chrysler's investment in the Chrysler Technology Center, the only place where the vehicle becomes whole. Stated Barry Price:

> We now have the ability to do everything from clay through vehicle testing, all at one facility; everything we need is right here, including the pilot plant for manufacturing and a track for vehicle testing. . . . This facility has been a *phenomenal tool.* We have gone from solving problems in months to solving them in days.[7]

Thus, Chrysler's ability to quickly coordinate interrelated activities, both internally and with suppliers, has increased dramatically in part due to creating a single location where the entire extended enterprise can jointly develop products.

In summary, the partner model has speed-to-market advantages relative to the arm's-length model due to: (1) reduced time spent on searching for, and contracting with, suppliers; (2) simultaneous versus sequential processing of work tasks; (3) additional time for suppliers to work out problems preproduction; and (4) dedicated coordination mechanisms that speed the flow of information.

Reduction in Product-Development Costs

Developing a new car model consists of four major costs: (1) engineering, research, and development (ER&D), or the costs of designing and engineering a new vehicle; (2) tools (e.g., dies, molds, etc.); (3) facilities (e.g., conveyors, presses, welding lines, etc.); and (4) pre-product launch (PP&L), which involves training and manufacturing preparation. On a typical Chrysler program, roughly 15–20 percent of total costs are ER&D, 40–45 percent are tools, 25–30 percent are facilities, and 5–10 percent PP&L. Since 1989, Chrysler has been able to significantly reduce overall program costs. Stated LH program manager Glenn Gardner:

> Cost control of both piece cost and investment has, in the past, been abysmal, and it was not uncommon to overrun budgets by more than 25 percent, and sometimes by as much as 50 percent in the investment category. The '93 LH was the first domestic

program that I have managed which came in under target. We brought the vehicle to market below the cost targets we committed to very early in the program. Also, you must remember the targets were very aggressive—stamping dies as an example were targeted at a 30 percent reduction compared to previous programs. As further proof that attainment of the LH cost objectives was not a fluke, I'm proud to say that the Neon and Ram pickup programs also beat their stringent objectives and our new Cirrus and Stratus will not spoil this string of below-budget achievements.[8]

Historical data suggest that the overall cost to develop a new vehicle has been gradually declining at Chrysler, with the LH program costing $1.6 billion, the Dodge Ram truck $1.3 billion, the Neon $1.2 billion, and the JA (Cirrus/Stratus) roughly $1 billion. Moreover, Chrysler's development costs have been considerably lower than GM's or Ford's for similar models. For example, GM's Saturn cost $3.5 billion to develop while Ford spent $2.5 billion to develop the Escort.[9] These cars are comparable to the Neon, which cost only $1.2 billion. Moreover, Ford reportedly spent $6 billion to develop the Mondeo/Contour, whereas Chrysler spent roughly $1 billion to develop the comparable Cirrus/Stratus.[10] It is important to note that these comparisons are not "apples-to-apples" comparisons due to differences in the items included in program costs for particular programs and automakers (e.g., some programs may involve building a new plant whereas others do not). However, the order of magnitude in these differences is noteworthy and consistent with the profitability and performance of these companies.

Chrysler's product-development costs have decreased due to reduced engineering hours spent on development due to a faster product-development cycle, delayed purchases of production (hard) tools, which saves on capital investments, and fewer changes in hard tools after they have been "cut" (produced). A faster product-development cycle (with the same engineering resources) means fewer engineering hours per vehicle. For example, on the LH (a $1.6 billion program) ER&D costs were roughly $300 million. By reducing ER&D time by 24 percent, Chrysler saved approximately $75 million. The new 1998 LH model saved an additional 10–15 percent in ER&D over the 1993 model.

A faster development cycle also reduces program costs because hard tools can be purchased closer to Job 1, or volume production. Historically, when the product-development cycle was slower, hard tools were purchased roughly 75–100 weeks before Job 1. However, now they are typically purchased between 50 to 60 weeks of Job 1. Thus, Chrysler saves 6–12 months of investment in hard tools. This is significant because Chrysler spent roughly $625 million on hard tools for the LH program. Thus, Chrysler saved approximately $62 million dollars on the LH program by delaying the purchase of hard tools (conservatively assuming a 10 percent cost of capital).

Chrysler has also saved money by reducing the number of changes in hard tools after they have been produced. Historically, the lengthy development process did not produce the first prototype until about 65 weeks before Job 1. However, the lead time on many hard tools was more than 65 weeks. Thus, hard tooling was started before the first prototype was completed. As a result, problems identified through the prototype had to be corrected after many of the hard tools had already been ordered. However, because suppliers were involved earlier on the LH program, the first prototype was completed 24 weeks earlier than previous programs. Thus, hard tools were not cut until *after* Chrysler and its suppliers had learned from the problems identified with the prototype. As a result, hard tool changes were fewer and Chrysler's investment in hard tools was lower. Moreover, fewer revisions are necessary late in the development program because the same supplier is now responsible for both the prototype part and the production part. Stated a Chrysler engineer:

> We used to have different suppliers for prototypes and final production. That often created problems because the final production parts would not work exactly like the prototype parts. The new system is faster because we cut the bureaucracy out and work together from the start. Communication is key. We save at least one year in tooling costs because we are faster than before. Also, we don't cut hard tools and then have to change them, which is expensive.[11]

In summary, the extended enterprise model economizes on product-development costs relative to the arm's-length model due to: reduced engineering hours, fewer costly revisions due to early supplier involvement, greater information sharing for joint problem solving, and delayed, or reduced, capital investments.

Production Cost Economies

Within most industries, as cumulative production experience in producing a product increases, quality is improved and costs are reduced. More specifically, each time accumulated production doubles, costs per unit typically fall (in real terms, adjusted for inflation) by 10 percent to 30 percent with comparable increases in quality.[12] By applying the partnership approach, Chrysler has consolidated its business with a few suppliers and created conditions that permit those suppliers to make the investments necessary to accelerate down the experience curve and to share the full advantage of this volume (and the resulting lower costs per unit) with Chrysler. When a supplier wins a contract with Chrysler it is essentially guaranteed business for the life of the model. Moreover, if the supplier performs up to expectations, it will usually win the business for the next model as well. The Chrysler suppliers I surveyed indicated that, on average, since 1990 they have had a 90-percent chance of re-winning the contract again when the model changes (see Figure 6.3). As a result, suppliers are more likely to make long-term plans and investments in the Chrysler relationship. Engineers from the two companies (Chrysler and its suppliers) are developing experience working together, making it easier to rapidly develop designs for the next car model. When the model change occurs, suppliers continue to move down the experience curve as depicted in Figure 6.3.

In contrast, General Motors has historically attempted to keep input prices low by maintaining size and bargaining power over suppliers. By splitting their business among many suppliers and rotating them frequently, GM has repeatedly destroyed the experience curves of suppliers by ensuring that no one supplier could accelerate down the experience curve to accumulate decisive cost advantages. The U.S. suppliers

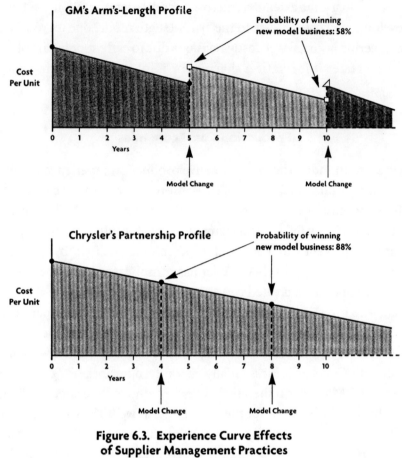

**Figure 6.3. Experience Curve Effects
of Supplier Management Practices**
(General Motors vs. Chrysler)

I surveyed reported that they have typically only had a 58-percent chance of re-winning GM's business at a model change. Thus, at each model change, the experience of the previous supplier is frequently destroyed and a new supplier must incur start-up costs. Moreover, suppliers are unable to effectively plan long-term production and investments, which is reflected in lower average plant capacity utilization. Without long-term commitments, GM's suppliers rationally refuse to make long-term investments in capital equipment. Moreover, without the ability to make long-term forecasts, it is very difficult to make maximum use of capacity and capital equipment.

Production costs also decrease within the extended enterprise because suppliers, who now have more control over design, can better utilize existing assets. Rather than create a unique new design for each model, suppliers may convince Chrysler to use some elements of a carryover design from the previous model, thereby more fully utilizing assets that suppliers have already acquired. In other cases, suppliers may offer Chrysler lower prices if it is willing to utilize a design similar to one that the supplier is producing for a Chrysler competitor. In other words, by not imposing a unique design on the supplier, Chrysler may be able to "free ride" on the investments that the supplier has made to produce a particular component for a Chrysler competitor. This allows for better utilization of assets within the extended enterprise.

Finally, production costs have decreased due to the SCORE program and the ideas that are generated through better information sharing within the extended enterprise. By giving suppliers cost-reduction targets and by creating methods for effective communication, Chrysler has generated enormous savings. Since SCORE's inception in 1990, SCORE savings have grown by more than 25 percent per year, and Chrysler realized over $2 billion in savings from SCORE in 1997 alone (see Figure 6.4).

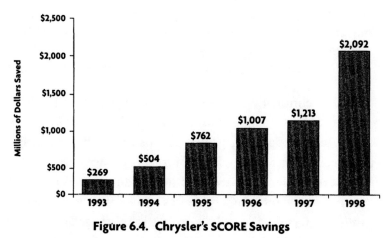

Figure 6.4. Chrysler's SCORE Savings

(*Source:* Chrysler Procurement and Supply)

Transaction-Cost (Procurement) Economies

Between 1988 and 1995, Chrysler reduced its number of buyers by 20 percent and dramatically increased (by 75 percent) the dollar value of goods procured per buyer. As Chrysler has grown, it has gradually added new buyers; but today Chrysler has only a few more buyers than it had in 1988 purchasing roughly twice the volume of product. Thus, Chrysler's transaction (procurement) costs have decreased substantially since adopting the partner model. Chrysler's transaction costs have decreased for *two primary reasons*. First, by reducing the number of overall suppliers Chrysler has lowered its search costs, or the costs associated with locating new suppliers and managing existing relationships with a large number of suppliers. Chrysler now searches within a smaller, restricted set of suppliers (typically two suppliers for a given product category) rather than across the universe of suppliers. This narrow search requires fewer resources for both Chrysler and its suppliers. In a presentation to suppliers in November 1994, Thomas Stallkamp requested that suppliers eliminate "sales reps" altogether and shift those resources into "program management" (i.e., engineering). The old way of doing business has become outdated. Stated one senior purchasing executive at Chrysler:

> Some sales reps are former professional athletes who walk in here with [Detroit] Pistons or Red Wing tickets in their back pockets. They are accustomed to schmoozing with buyers to give their company an edge. But now they are dinosaurs. They don't have the skills we need to be productive. I almost feel sorry for them.[13]

Second, by eliminating competitive bidding Chrysler has lowered negotiation and contracting costs. Fewer resources are devoted to contracting because suppliers trust that payoffs will be divided fairly over the long run. Furthermore, costly contracts may not even be written, or if they are written they are for a longer duration. As a result, as demonstrated in chapter 4, Chrysler has lower transaction costs (fewer procurement personnel per dollar of parts purchased) than GM or Ford. (Recall that the dollar value of goods procured per procurement employee in 1994 was $6.4 million for Chrysler, $5.4 million for Ford, and $1.8 million for GM.) Moreover, Chrysler's suppliers' transaction costs are also relatively low. In a survey of 38 major first-tier U.S. suppliers, they reported that they spent 21 percent of their face-to-face contact time with Chrysler on price and contract negotiations and assigning blame for problems. These are non-value-added activities that represent transaction costs. By comparison, the comparable numbers for GM and Ford were 47 and 30 percent respectively. Thus, suppliers report significantly lower transaction costs when working with Chrysler than with GM or Ford.

Improvements in Quality

During the past 20 years, Chrysler has been known for producing the least reliable, or lowest quality, cars among the U.S. automakers. The reputation was warranted. Between 1988 and 1991, Chrysler's problems per 100 vehicles, as measured by J.D. Power and Associates, were approximately 20 percent higher than GM and 25 percent higher than Ford (see Figure 6.5). Various reasons have been offered for Chrysler's inferior quality, including fewer engineering resources and less capable "systems integration" skills. However, Chrysler's supplier management practices were certainly a big part of the problem. To illustrate, in the mid 1980s, Bain & Company conducted a study for Chrysler on sourcing. In one area studied, wiring harnesses (electrical wiring), Bain found that Chrysler used more than 20 different suppliers. Not

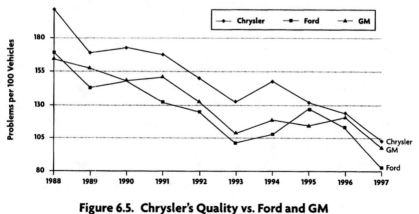

Figure 6.5. Chrysler's Quality vs. Ford and GM

(*Source:* J.D. Power Initial Quality Data, 1988–1997)

surprisingly, the costs associated with managing these suppliers was extremely high and communication with each was poor. But perhaps more importantly, the short-term orientation created an incentive for suppliers to scrimp on quality, and tracking quality problems was a nightmare for Chrysler. When more suppliers are used for a given part, variation increases and reliability goes down. As quality guru W. Edwards Deming once noted, "Even with a single supplier, there is substantial variation lot-to-lot and within lots."[14] Using multiple suppliers only increases the variation of parts that causes production problems and poor quality.

Largely as a result of an increased emphasis on quality and superior communication with a smaller set of partner suppliers, Chrysler's quality has been gradually improving. In fact, from 1990 to 1997 Chrysler has reduced its defects by more than 40 percent. As a result, according to J.D. Power and Associates, Chrysler's initial quality (as measured in problems per 100 vehicles) is now virtually identical to the quality achieved by General Motors and Ford.

Increases in Market Share and Profitability

Historically car model sales (in units) have increased substantially in both the United States and Japan after a major model change.[15] Thus, automakers who are able to develop new models more quickly than competitors have an advantage because their current models are more advanced and include the latest in technology.[16] Consequently, we would expect Chrysler's ability to produce more new models more efficiently to result in higher market share and profitability. In fact, Chrysler's market share in the U.S. car and truck market has increased from 12.2 percent in 1988 to 16.1 percent in 1998, its highest share in 25 years (see Table 6.1). Chrysler's profitability has also improved dramatically. Chrysler's return on assets, which was traditionally lower than competitors throughout the 1980s, has been the highest among U.S. automakers since 1992. Moreover, its profit per unit (vehicle) has increased from an average of approximately $250 per unit in the 1980s (1985–1989 average) to roughly $2,000 per unit since 1992. This represents a tenfold increase in profit performance.

Table 6.1. Chrysler Profit and Market Share Performance
Relative to Ford and General Motors (1988–1998)

Performance Measure	1988	1989	1990	1991	1992	1993	1994	1995	1996	1997	1998
1. Return on Assets (%)											
Chrysler	3.5	1.1	0.3	–1.9	2.3	8.8	11.8	9.8	15.0	9.5	11.1
Ford	5.8	3.7	0.8	–0.1	–1.4	2.0	8.5	4.5	3.2	8.2	7.5
GM	5.4	5.1	–1.3	–1.8	–3.1	1.3	6.9	6.7	4.3	0.0	2.8
2. Profit per Unit ($)											
Chrysler	649	249	209	(427)	445	1,709	2,110	1,290	2,059	1,468	2,055
Ford	1014	663	53	(700)	(307)	240	775	479	378	1,000	1,019
GM	684	645	(462)	(883)	(541)	208	270	594	542	683	312
3. Market Share (%)											
Chrysler	13.9	13.7	13.2	12.2	12.2	14.7	14.6	14.7	16.2	15.1	16.1
Ford	23.7	24.6	23.8	22.8	24.6	25.6	25.3	25.8	25.8	25.2	24.6
GM	34.9	35.0	35.5	35.1	33.9	33.4	33.1	32.6	30.9	31.0	28.9

(*Sources:* Figures derived from companies' annual reports and Chilton's Automotive Industries report card issues)

Risks Associated with Chrysler's Extended Enterprise

By now a thoughtful reader will suspect that this is too good to be true. It seems as though the extended enterprise model offers only an upside with no downside, greater profits without any risks. This is a reasonable, and appropriate, concern. As is true with many bold strategic initiatives, while the overall benefits of the partner model appear to outweigh the costs, it does not come without some risks. My interviews at Chrysler and with suppliers revealed two important risks associated with moving to the extended enterprise model. The first involves the risks associated with handing off additional responsibilities to suppliers. The risk arises because a new process creates confusion regarding who is responsible for what. Under the arm's-length model, there is a high degree of clarity regarding responsibilities. However, as Chrysler transfers more design, testing, and manufacturing responsibilities to suppliers, it is less clear whether Chrysler or its suppliers are responsible for coordinating various functions (especially across suppliers). As a result, design changes made in one component or component system that affect the performance of another component or system may not be effectively communicated, thereby creating fit or quality problems.

One of the reasons that it has taken a few years for Chrysler's quality to substantially improve is that Chrysler and its partner suppliers were learning their responsibilities and roles. Even today, a more decentralized extended enterprise structure makes it more difficult for Chrysler to achieve the tight integration necessary to achieve a high degree of product integrity. Chrysler will need to continue to work on this if it hopes to further eliminate quality problems.

The second risk arises from Chrysler's increased dependence on a smaller group of suppliers that have become more powerful (and, in a real sense, have more bargaining power). As a result, Chrysler is more vulnerable if suppliers decide to behave opportunistically. In order for Chrysler to benefit from the extended enterprise model, suppliers must buy into the process, behave in a trustworthy manner, and create benefits through cost-reduction ideas, innovations, and responsiveness—all value-creation initiatives that cannot be specified in a legal contract. Thus, the process for getting value out of suppliers is very different from the process used to extract value from suppliers in an arm's-length model. As Chrysler's Barry Price acknowledged: "We know that on any given day we can bid one of our parts in the marketplace and find a lower price. But that will destroy the trust we have developed with suppliers and will not give us the lowest costs over the long run."[17] For the partnership model to work effectively, both Chrysler and its suppliers must invest in non-contractible items, such as information sharing, responsiveness, and innovative ideas, in order to optimize the performance of the value chain. If suppliers are unwilling or unable to do this, then the extended enterprise model will be ineffective at creating competitive advantages for the participating firms.

Conclusion

In this chapter I examined how, due largely to its extended enterprise, Chrysler has increased its profits by a factor of 10. More specifically, Chrysler has reduced its product-development cycle by 35 percent and now has speed-to-market capabilities that exceed its U.S. and European competitors. At the same time, it has cut product development costs by 20 to 40 percent and reduced production and transaction costs to the point where it has the lowest cost structure of the Big Three. This is particularly impressive since Ford and GM have significant economies of scale advantages over Chrysler. Further, Chrysler has improved its initial quality from roughly two problems per vehicle in 1990 to approximately one problem per vehicle in 1997.[18] In short, Chrysler has made extraordinary improvements on virtually every measure of performance. Chrysler's experience convincingly demonstrates the awesome power that can be unleashed when a group of companies truly collaborate as an effective team. Establishing an extended enterprise is not easy, but the rewards can be enormous. For those executives who want further guidance on how to successfully establish an extended enterprise of their own, chapter 7 builds on the blueprint offered in chapter 5. In the next chapter we examine three additional keys to successfully implementing the extended enterprise concept.

7

Key Lessons for Implementing
the Extended Enterprise

> We are simply an extension of Toyota. It's like we are the same company.
> —Sales vice president, Toyota supplier

In the preceding chapters I carefully examined the key elements of the extended enterprises established by Toyota and Chrysler. I also described how and why Toyota and Chrysler have been able to create competitive advantages through effective collaboration with their supplier networks. Although I have attempted to provide extensive detail on the process Chrysler used to transform its adversarial supplier relationships into partnerships, executives who are intrigued by the extended enterprise concept still may have many unanswered questions. For example, I am frequently asked the following types of questions: What are the general lessons that executives can glean from these examples to assist them in developing their own extended enterprises? What are the guiding principles for implementation? What are the future directions of the extended enterprise? The purpose of this chapter is to offer some general answers to the first two questions. The third will be addressed in the final chapter.

The experience of Toyota (in the United States) and Chrysler in establishing their extended enterprises suggests that—at a broad strategic level—a few factors were critical to their success. What follows is a discussion of three key lessons for executives who are interested in creating collaborative advantage with their value chain partners.

Carefully Select Enterprise Members:
Strategically Segment Suppliers

Executives who want to establish an extended enterprise typically begin the process with the following question: Which other companies should be included in extended enterprise activities? Should all suppliers be included? Should only the most important first-tier suppliers? Technically, all suppliers in an assembler's value chain are in the extended enterprise, but not all have the same capability to create value—and competitive advantage—for the extended enterprise. Furthermore, developing partnerships takes considerable time, effort, and resources. Consequently, a firm should first determine which suppliers should be partners in its governance profile, and then begin to establish an extended enterprise by inviting those firms to participate. For example, Toyota's efforts to create an extended enterprise began by focusing on its affiliated (*kankei kaisha*) suppliers, or those partner suppliers in which Toyota had taken a stock-ownership position. Why did Toyota take stock-ownership positions in some suppliers and not others? The answer appears to be that affiliated suppliers are more likely to provide strategic inputs whereas independent suppliers (*dokuritsu kaisha*) provide non-strategic inputs. By *strategic* I mean those high-value inputs that may be useful in differentiating the final assembler's product. For example, Toyota's affiliated suppliers (e.g., Denso and Aishin Seiki) produce the following types of components: transmission and engine parts, air conditioners, body and instrument panels, and seats. These parts are customized to the car model and help differentiate the model from competitor offerings. Non-strategic parts are those parts such as rubber hoses and belts, tires, batteries, and fasteners that are not customized and do not differentiate the car model. These parts are produced by non-affiliated suppliers, such as Mitsuboshi Belting (rubber hoses and belts) and Bridgestone (tires).

Interestingly, though not surprisingly, I found that Toyota provided significantly more assistance to affiliated suppliers to help them lower production costs, improve quality, and minimize inventories. Although all of Toyota's suppliers received assistance and trusted Toyota to a high degree, Toyota's affiliated suppliers shared more information, had twice as much face-to-face contact, and received roughly 30 percent more assistance from Toyota when compared with independent suppliers. In short, Toyota focused much greater effort and resources on its affiliated suppliers, or those suppliers that it viewed as its strategic partners.

Thus, when initiating an extended enterprise, suppliers should be analyzed and then segmented into at least two groups: one group that provides necessary but non-strategic inputs, and another group that provides strategic inputs. This often requires a process of mapping out the supply chain to visualize the enterprise and identify risks and opportunities in the supply chain. Then, the orchestrator of the extended enterprise activities should focus its time and resources on creating collaborative advantage with the firms providing strategic, high-value inputs. Chrysler has done this to some degree by identifying its top 150 strategic suppliers (determined mostly by the value of the supplier's inputs). Chrysler has an annual meeting with those suppliers and also meets with them individually (quarterly) to review priorities and evaluate performance. It would be difficult and costly to devote the same resources to its entire supply base of roughly 1,000 suppliers. But in my opinion, even Chrysler could go further in identifying which of its 150 suppliers provide the most critical and strategic inputs. By focusing initially on strategic suppliers, the buying firm can better leverage its resources. Moreover, since strategic suppliers offer more potential to create collaborative advantage, achieving success with those suppliers will serve as a pilot for extending the ideas to other suppliers (much the way Chrysler used the LH vehicle program to demonstrate the value of the partnership approach to the entire Chrysler organization). Successful pilots will help break down organizational resistance to implementing extended enterprise ideas throughout the organization. To enhance the probability of success, it is important to understand how to select, and manage, strategic partners.

Selecting and Managing Strategic Partners

Partnerships are critical when suppliers provide strategic inputs. Generally speaking, these inputs are not subject to industry standards and, therefore, can be customized to a particular customer's product. In fact, they may have to be customized if the component has an inter-action or system effect with other components in the final product. In contrast, for inputs that are necessary, but non-strategic, firms should employ quasi-arm's-length relationships (I will discuss this momen-tarily). Non-strategic inputs require a low degree of supplier-buyer interdependence and coordination. Consequently, there is little need for investments in dedicated assets. In addition, the value added by non-strategic components is likely to be lower than for strategic inputs. Thus, they have less ability to influence the cost (value) of the final product.

Because strategic inputs are more likely to be customized (to achieve higher quality, new features, etc.), they require a high degree of coor-dination between supplier and buyer. Thus, strategic partnerships require multiple function-to-function interfaces between the supplier and buyer. For example, a strategic supplier's design engineers must coordinate with buyer design engineers to ensure flawless product fit and smooth interfaces. The buyer's sales organization must share mar-keting information with the supplier's sales and product-development functions to ensure that the supplier clearly understands the final cus-tomer's needs and the role of their component or subsystem in the overall product strategy. Buyer manufacturing engineers must coor-dinate with supplier engineers to ensure that the supplier's product can be easily assembled at the buyer's plant. Not surprisingly, dedi-cated investments are necessary in order for the supplying firm to cus-tomize the component and coordinate effectively with the buying firm. These include investments in dedicated plants and equipment, dedi-cated personnel, and tailored manufacturing processes. It is not unusual for a Toyota affiliated supplier in Japan to have a plant tai-lored and almost entirely dedicated to Toyota.

Due to multiple functional interfaces and dedicated asset invest-ments, organizational boundaries between supplier and buyer begin to blur. The partners' destinies become tightly intertwined and a shared identity begins to emerge. Thus, each party has strong incentives to help the other as much as possible. This explains why Toyota provides such high levels of assistance to their affiliated suppliers—because its success is highly dependent on the success of its affiliated suppliers.

Consequently, creating knowledge-sharing routines that transfer know-how and technology to partner suppliers is important because it is imperative that Toyota's affiliated suppliers have world-class capabilities. Similarly, partner suppliers must be willing to exert efforts at innovation and quality and be responsive in ways that go beyond the explicit requirements of the contract.

In terms of managing strategic partnerships, the buying firm must be effective at: (1) *capabilities benchmarking* (analyzing suppliers' cost structure and engineering capabilities) to ensure that the best possible partners are chosen, (2) developing trust so that partners will be willing to share knowledge and make investments in dedicated assets, and (3) creating interfirm knowledge-sharing routines to effectively coordinate activities and facilitate knowledge transfers.

I previously alluded to the idea that non-strategic suppliers should be managed as quasi-arm's-length relationships—at least if the firm wants to involve them in the extended enterprise. Alternatively, they can be managed as pure arm's-length relationships and not really be involved in the extended enterprise. The quasi-arm's-length model differs from the traditional arm's-length model in the following respects. First, initial supplier selection requires some capabilities benchmarking to determine which suppliers have the potential for the lowest costs over the long term. Then, three to four suppliers can be selected to be long-term suppliers in a given product category (it is important to keep the number of suppliers down to reduce administrative costs and keep a manageable number of suppliers in the extended enterprise; also, dividing purchases across multiple suppliers reduces the ability of suppliers to achieve significant economies of scale). The traditional arm's-length model simply opens up the bidding to all suppliers without regard for their capabilities or the costs of working with and managing a large group of suppliers.

Second, the supplier and buyer make *some* dedicated investments in interfirm coordination mechanisms, such as order-entry systems, electronic data exchange, and logistics systems, which will get the product to the buyer where and when the buyer needs it. In the traditional arm's-length model, all such investments are avoided.

Finally, the supplier is assured of some future business as long as prices are competitive. Relatively frequent price benchmarking is necessary to maintain vigorous price competition between the suppliers. For example, the buyer may create some automatic reorder dates (e.g., once a year) at which time suppliers must rebid for business. Bidding and reordering can also be carried out electronically according to pre-announced criteria so that procurement administrative costs can be kept to a minimum. The frequent price benchmarking (bids) keeps suppliers on their toes—they know they must continually offer low prices. However, they are willing to make the necessary investments in coordination mechanisms, logistics, and distribution processes because they have a long-term commitment for at least some business.

Online bidding auctions are ideal for arm's-length relationships in which suppliers are providing pure commodities. These can be done by the enterprise alone or in concert with other extended enterprises, as is the case with GM, Ford, and Chrysler with their newly created Internet Parts Exchange. Of course, collaborating with other firms or extended enterprises requires that each enterprise be willing to use the identical supplies. In many instances this will be the ideal way to achieve the lowest costs, though if firms are collaborating with competitors it will not create competitive advantages for any single firm.

In summary, the quasi-arm's-length approach may be superior to the traditional arm's-length approach because it minimizes procurement (transaction) costs; allows suppliers to maximize economies of scale, which is critical in standardized, commodity-like products; and maintains vigorous competition. Buyers may also reopen the business to all bidders at longer time intervals (e.g., every two years), to ensure that their long-term suppliers still have the lowest costs and best capabilities. The price benchmarking (and open bidding) intervals should be shorter the more commodity-like the product and the greater the environmental and technological uncertainty regarding the factors that influence the cost structure of suppliers (i.e., the more frequently suppliers' production costs are likely to change). Because arm's-length suppliers provide inputs that are less able to differentiate the buyer's product, there will naturally be a much greater focus on price than there will be with strategic suppliers.

Finally, it is worth noting that a greater percentage of suppliers will be strategic partners: (1) in complex-product industries, where the demands of complexity increase the value of effective interfirm coordination; (2) during a long-term economic (industry) expansion, when scarcity of resources may be a problem; and (3) when long-term value creation (e.g., through quality, new technologies, etc.) is the goal. In contrast, quasi-arm's-length relationships may be more desirable: (1) in simple product industries or industries with high levels of standardization of components, (2) in declining industries where suppliers have chronic excess capacity due to exit barriers and high fixed costs, and (3) when short-term cost reduction is the primary goal. (See Figure 7.1 for a comparison of the conditions under which it makes sense to manage suppliers in partnership fashion versus an arm's-length fashion.) However, vacillating between arm's-length relationships and partnerships with suppliers is unlikely to be a successful strategy given the long-term commitment and dedicated investments required for strategic partnerships to be successful. As General Motors has discovered, companies that violate partnership agreements will develop a reputation for behaving opportunistically and, therefore, will have great difficulty in convincing suppliers to make the investments necessary for strategic partnerships to work effectively.

In summary, given the level of resources required to generate value through partnerships, a firm desiring to establish an extended enterprise may need to be selective and focus its energies primarily on

Quasi-Arm's-Length Model	Partnership Model
• Low volumes of exchange (buy low percentage of supplier's output)	• High volumes of exchange
• One-time or infrequent purchases	• Recurring purchases
• Low degree of supplier-buyer interdependence; low ability to affect each other's costs	• High degree of supplier-buyer interdependence; high ability to affect each other's costs
• Stand-alone inputs (no or few interaction effects with other inputs)	• Inputs with multiple interaction effects with other inputs
• During a recession (when suppliers have excess capacity)	• During an expansion (when inputs are scarce)
• Short-term cost reduction is the goal	• Long-term value creation is the goal (speed-to-market, quality, new technology)

Figure 7.1. Conditions Under Which Each Model Will Be More Effective

developing partnerships with those companies that bring high-value, customized inputs that interact with other components and systems. After effectively involving those suppliers with the potential to create the greatest value, the firm can then gradually extend the size and scope of its extended enterprise.

Create an Identity for the Extended Enterprise

The second lesson in creating an extended enterprise is to discover ways to get the partner firms within your extended enterprise to identify with the larger collective. In short, it is important to get a team of firms to behave as though they are part of the same firm—with a shared sense of purpose and common objectives. Of course, this is a challenge because individual firms are inclined to behave in a self-interested manner and do not want to subjugate their narrow interests for the good of the whole. That is one key reason that firms are superior to markets (arm's-length relationships) at coordination, communication, and learning.[1] Another reason that firms are better than markets at coordination, communication, and learning is because these activities are situated not only physically in locality, but also mentally in an identity. Let me explain what I mean by *identity*.

Creating an identity for a collective (e.g., firm, extended enterprise) means that the individual members feel a shared sense of social community and a shared sense of purpose with the collective. The identity of the firm is defined by the organizational boundaries which dictate who is (and who is not) a member of the organization, by shared goals and values, and by patterns of interaction among individuals that give rise to a common language and common frameworks for action.[2] For example, as a member of a firm I belong to a social community within that firm, and I am likely to feel a shared sense of purpose with other individuals in the firm as we strive to achieve common objectives. Because I identify with the firm, I am likely to behave in ways that will be in the best interests of the firm. When someone within the firm requests information or assistance, I offer it voluntarily without engaging in costly negotiations or in a cost-benefit calculus. It becomes automatic. This shared identity not only lowers the costs of communication, but also establishes explicit and tacit rules of coordination within the firm.[3] Thus, knowledge is most effectively generated, combined, and transferred by individuals who cooperate in a social community. And knowledge is a powerful weapon for creating competitive advantage.

While these arguments are applicable to firms, they are equally applicable to the extended enterprise. However, it is more difficult to create an identity for a network of firms because the firm is the "unit of accrual" for performance and success.[4] Profits are accrued and reported at the firm level. Stock markets measure the value of individual firms, not networks of firms. Consequently, it is difficult to change one's mindset from the firm to the extended enterprise as the unit of analysis for establishing competitive advantage. But if an extended enterprise can create a shared identity among members—a shared social community and shared sense of purpose—then that shared identity can lower the costs of coordination, communication, and knowledge sharing within the enterprise. Furthermore, the diversity of knowledge that resides within the extended enterprise is much greater than that which resides in a single firm. Consequently, if the extended enterprise can get its members to cooperate in a social community, it will produce learning and value-creation opportunities far superior to firms that do not reside within such a network.

To illustrate, Toyota's extended enterprise in Japan is effective at collaborating (especially knowledge sharing) largely because a strong enterprise identity has emerged, and the enterprise has established rules that support coordination, communication, and learning. In Japan, Toyota's network is known as the Toyota Group, and Toyota openly promotes a philosophy within the Toyota Group called "co-existence and co-prosperity" (*kyoson kyoei* in Japanese). Toyota has also promoted this philosophy to its U.S. suppliers. According to Koichiro Noguchi, former head of international purchasing at Toyota: "We must have the best suppliers in the industry. We rely on them for our success. Quality cars require quality suppliers."[5] This sentiment was echoed by a Toyota supplier executive in Japan who stated that: "Toyota truly believes in *kyoson kyoei*. Its not just a slogan. They are true believers." This executive unknowingly acknowledged that his company had internalized the philosophy when he commented that, "As a Toyota supplier, we know that our success is tied to Toyota's."

This philosophy is critical to making an extended enterprise successful. Member firms cannot be constantly arguing for their individual self-interests. The Toyota *kyoson kyoei* philosophy is similar to making the argument that "what is good for the extended enterprise is good for me; and what is good for me is good for the extended enterprise." (This is reminiscent of former General Motors President Charles Wilson, who reportedly said, "What's good for our country is good for General Motors, and vice versa.")[6] The fact that Toyota's suppliers have truly internalized this philosophy makes it much easier for the extended enterprise to collaborate to create competitive advantage.

In similar fashion, Chrysler has attempted to create an identity for its extended enterprise. Indeed, Chrysler executives coined, and even trademarked, the phrase "extended enterprise" in an attempt to get suppliers to identify with its initiatives. Chrysler tells its partner suppliers (particularly its largest 150 strategic suppliers) that they "belong" to its extended enterprise. Chrysler defines its extended enterprise as follows:

> A unified group of suppliers and supply tiers who strive together to maximize the effectiveness of vehicle development and minimize total system costs in order to maximize the value passed on to a common ultimate customer.[7]

The emphasis here is on a *unified* group effort to *maximize* the effectiveness of vehicle development and *minimize* total system costs. Thus, Chrysler tries to get suppliers to buy in to the idea that individual firm objectives and subgoals are less important than the performance and goals of the entire system. Let me offer one brief illustration of how this philosophy can influence supplier behavior.

Magna International, a supplier of a wide variety of automotive components, is one of the suppliers that Chrysler has chosen to work with in partnership fashion. During the past seven years, Magna's sales to Chrysler have more than tripled as Chrysler has consolidated its suppliers. Thus, Chrysler has become a much more important customer to Magna and, likewise, Magna has become a much more important supplier to Chrysler. In fact, as Chrysler was developing its next generation minivan (launched in 1997), Magna played a significant role, supplying more than $900 of parts on every minivan. Thus, the minivan was extremely important to *both* Chrysler's and Magna's success. A few months before volume production a couple of Chrysler's suppliers were experiencing difficulties in production that threatened to delay the launch of the minivan. According to former purchasing chief Thomas Stallkamp, Magna came to the rescue.

> Magna knew they had a lot at stake in the minivan, and they were willing to do what was necessary to make it a success. So they sent their engineers to the suppliers that were having production problems to help them solve the problems so that the launch would not be delayed. They were able to help the suppliers fix the problems, and we met our launch objectives.... This is an example of the value of our extended enterprise.[8]

Thus, Magna was willing to devote its resources to helping other members of the extended enterprise because it recognized its interdependence with those suppliers. If an extended enterprise can inculcate this philosophy among its members, then this opens up a wide array of opportunities for collaboration—and competitive advantage.

Both Toyota and Chrysler have used the co-location of personnel within the extended enterprise (e.g., resident engineers) to create an identity for the collective. By 1999, both companies had more than 700 supplier resident engineers at their technical centers. Moreover, Toyota transfers many of its employees to work at suppliers. Thus, job rotations occur within Toyota's extended enterprise, not at the firm level. The fact that individuals can be transferred across firm boundaries indicates that the unit of analysis for a job rotation is not the individual firm, but the extended enterprise. Employee training is also frequently done at the enterprise level rather than the firm level. In fact, Toyota's supplier association provides a significant amount of training for engineers at both Toyota and its suppliers.

As a final example of the importance Toyota places on communication with, and among, suppliers, Toyota recently built a Supplier Center next to its headquarters and technical center in Toyota City, Japan. The new five-floor building, completed in 1998 to commemorate the fiftieth anniversary of Toyota's supplier association (*kyohokai*), has display rooms for suppliers' products as well as meeting rooms to be used for suppliers, association meetings, and so forth. Thus, the building is an extended enterprise building, not a Toyota building. The building represents not only Toyota's commitment to working closely with its suppliers, but is a symbol of Toyota's reliance on the Toyota Group of companies which make it a success.

Be Patient:
The Enterprise Needs Time to Emerge and Evolve

Finally, it is important to understand that creating an extended enterprise takes time. Collaborative advantage does not materialize overnight. To illustrate, Toyota's extended enterprise in Japan has been more than 50 years in the making. Toyota's supplier association in Japan has been in existence for more than 50 years, its consulting division (OMCD) for more than 25 years, its *jishuken* groups for more than 20 years. Chrysler's extended enterprise has made remarkable progress in just 10 years—but it took at least 2–3 years before its extended enterprise began to pay dividends. Since the advantages of the extended enterprise are largely derived from value-creation activities (such as innovation, flexibility, speed, quality) rather than pure cost reduction (lower unit costs), the orchestrator of the enterprise must put the appropriate processes in place and patiently wait for the enterprise to evolve into a value-creation machine. It will not create value overnight because some of the key ingredients—trust, for example—cannot be created instantaneously. To illustrate how an extended enterprise can be created, and how it may evolve, I will briefly examine Toyota's experience in establishing an extended enterprise in the United States. Toyota has been in the process of establishing its extended enterprise in the United States for the last 10 years, but has only started to reap substantial benefits in the last 3–5 years.

Phase 1: Developing Relationships
and an Enterprise Identity

In 1988, when Toyota first began producing cars in Georgetown, Kentucky, its U.S. suppliers barely knew Toyota and they certainly did not interact with each other. Collaboration within the supplier network was virtually nonexistent. The first step that Toyota took to initiate knowledge sharing in the supplier network was to establish its supplier association (BAMA) in 1989. The supplier association was designed to facilitate the sharing of explicit knowledge (mostly unidirectional flows from Toyota to suppliers) and the creation of social ties among suppliers. But amazingly, only 13 suppliers initially joined. However, Toyota continued unfazed. They invested in the supplier association's activities and made sure that the activities were valuable to the small number of suppliers who did choose to participate. Gradually, the word spread and new suppliers joined. By 1998 the association had grown to include 100 suppliers, and membership in the association had become highly valued by suppliers. Creating an association (and the opportunity for suppliers to get together to build a social community) was a critical first step in getting members of the network to talk to each other in a non-threatening setting. It was also a critical step in creating an identity for the extended enterprise. According to Toyota's Chris Nielsen, assistant general manager for purchasing planning:

> BAMA was the catalyst for getting suppliers to talk to each other. Before BAMA, it was not very natural for supplier executives to talk and share information.[9]

This message was echoed by the plant manager of a Toyota supplier.

> Before BAMA, we really didn't know or share information with executives at other suppliers. And we just didn't think about calling them up or visiting. It just didn't happen. BAMA has helped us to get to know each other and now it feels a lot more comfortable calling up another supplier for information or even visiting their plants.[10]

Thus, BAMA was the catalyst for creating relationships among suppliers, and it created an avenue for sharing explicit, non-proprietary knowledge. Suppliers felt comfortable participating because they were not required to share sensitive information or commit significant resources.

Phase 2: Developing Strong Ties with Toyota

Three years after establishing its supplier association, Toyota made its well-trained consultants available (free of charge) to transfer valuable knowledge regarding the Toyota Production System (TPS) at the suppliers' facilities. The Toyota consultants were the catalysts for creating a norm of reciprocity and a feeling of indebtedness and openness within the supplier network. Indeed, to receive assistance from Toyota consultants the supplier had to agree to open up its plant to other Toyota suppliers. As the vice president of planning for Summit Polymers, a supplier of plastic interior parts, stated:

> I couldn't believe it but Toyota sent approximately two to four consultants *every day* for a period of three to four months as we implemented Toyota Production System concepts in a new plant. They gave us a valuable gift [the Toyota Production System]. Naturally we feel indebted towards Toyota and view them as a special customer; they sincerely want to help us improve.... How could we try to keep what we've learned from other Toyota suppliers?[11]

Thus, the consulting assistance helped Toyota establish much stronger direct relationships with suppliers and was the catalyst for creating a norm of reciprocal obligation. As more and more suppliers had an intensive knowledge-transfer experience with Toyota's consultants (typically over a one- to two-year period), they became comfortable with knowledge-transfer activities and came to trust Toyota. Moreover, an increasing number of suppliers were obligated to allow visits from other suppliers in the network, thereby setting the stage for the development of strong relationships among suppliers.

Phase 3: Developing Strong Ties Among Suppliers

After a large number of suppliers had realized performance improvements due to Toyota's assistance, Toyota divided suppliers into small learning teams (like the *jishuken* teams in Japan described in chapter 4). Toyota carefully organized the teams to maximize the willingness and ability of suppliers to learn from each other (e.g., they put direct competitors in different teams). By doing so, Toyota created a set of subnetworks within the full extended enterprise. These subnetworks were designed to facilitate the creation of strong relationships among suppliers, which in turn has facilitated the sharing of tacit (confidential) knowledge among suppliers. Stated the plant manager of a wheel trim supplier:

> We've benefited greatly by participating in the "blue" (PDA core) group. It is now very natural for us to share what we know with the other suppliers in our group. We know each other well and are committed to helping each other.... I don't know that I could have imagined this sort of activity five years ago. We just didn't interact with other suppliers.[12]

Not only have strong relationships developed through the formal PDA core group activities, strong ties and avenues for knowledge sharing have also developed informally. Stated the plant manager of another supplier:

> We don't just visit "core group" [*jishuken*] members. In fact, one of our most helpful visits was to Tower [a supplier of small metal stampings]. We heard that Tower had one of the best *kanban* systems, so we asked them if we could visit and see what they do. We had a very productive visit.[13]

Thus, over time Toyota's production network has become increasingly interconnected as suppliers have developed relationships with each other. The result is that the extended enterprise relies less on Toyota to direct and facilitate the knowledge-sharing activities. States Toyota's Nielsen: "We want our suppliers to help each other. That's the whole idea. We simply don't have the resources or information to help all our suppliers as much as we'd like to."[14]

In summary, Toyota's U.S. supplier network, which initially did not function as an effective extended enterprise, has evolved and changed substantially over time. During the initiation phase the enterprise structure was essentially a collection of dyadic ties with Toyota as a hub heavily subsidizing enterprise activities (see Figure 7.2). Toyota's subsidies came in two forms: financial (money for meeting rooms, social activities, organizing and planning meetings) and valuable knowledge (the consulting division, TSSC, and free consultants for participating members). It was important for Toyota to subsidize extended-enterprise activities early on to motivate members to participate and to ensure that they realized sufficient benefits from participation.

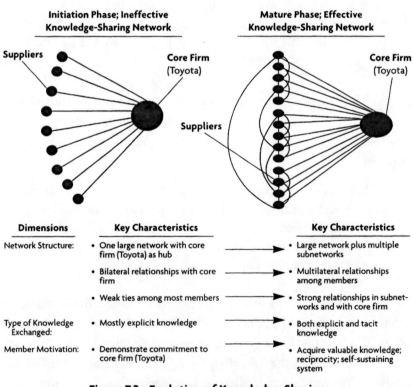

Dimensions	Key Characteristics		Key Characteristics
Network Structure:	• One large network with core firm (Toyota) as hub	⟶	• Large network plus multiple subnetworks
	• Bilateral relationships with core firm	⟶	• Multilateral relationships among members
	• Weak ties among most members	⟶	• Strong relationships in subnetworks and with core firm
Type of Knowledge Exchanged:	• Mostly explicit knowledge	⟶	• Both explicit and tacit knowledge
Member Motivation:	• Demonstrate commitment to core firm (Toyota)	⟶	• Acquire valuable knowledge; reciprocity; self-sustaining system

Figure 7.2. Evolution of Knowledge-Sharing in Toyota's U.S. Extended Enterprise

However, Toyota gradually built strong and trusting relationships with suppliers through the one-to-one knowledge transfers (consultants) and the supplier association activities. Suppliers began to receive valuable knowledge at minimal cost. Consequently, suppliers increasingly participated in the network not only to demonstrate their commitment to Toyota, but also to receive the knowledge transfers from Toyota. During this phase the network began to take on a stronger identity. Suppliers began to feel an increased obligation to Toyota and began to identify more strongly with the extended enterprise's social community.

The final phase in the evolutionary process was to strengthen multilateral ties among suppliers and develop multiple subnetworks for knowledge sharing within the larger extended enterprise. This was accomplished largely through the learning team processes, which strengthened multilateral ties, thereby facilitating tacit knowledge sharing among suppliers. Thus, enterprise-level knowledge-sharing processes have become self-sustaining in the sense that suppliers willingly participate without doing it simply to show loyalty to Toyota. Suppliers now identify with the Toyota production network, and their routines for helping other suppliers in the network have become automatic and, in effect, involuntary. Further, there are multiple mechanisms and pathways for transferring both explicit and tacit knowledge, with tacit knowledge being exchanged primarily in the subnetworks and through the one-to-one transfers. In this mature phase of the extended enterprise, the degree of tacit knowledge being transferred is substantial whereas it was almost nonexistent in the initiation phase. Not surprisingly, since tacit knowledge is typically more valuable than explicit knowledge, suppliers benefit more by participating in the extended enterprise.

Again, let me emphasize that it took Toyota at least three to five years before the extended enterprise began creating measurable value. Toyota patiently implemented the key processes and nurtured the activities that encouraged the voluntary and energetic participation of its suppliers. It is now reaping the rewards for its patience, having developed a group of suppliers in the United States that produce components at lower costs, and with fewer defects, for Toyota than for Toyota's U.S. competitors.

Conclusion

In this chapter I identified three factors that play an important role in the successful establishment of an extended enterprise. First, I examined the criteria that firms should use in identifying and selecting suppliers for participation in the extended enterprise. Given the high level of resources required to generate value through partnerships, a firm desiring to establish an extended enterprise may need to be selective and initially focus its energies on developing partnerships with those companies that bring high value, customized inputs that interact with other components and systems. Second, I discussed the importance of designing a set of processes, activities, and socialization initiatives that create an identity for the extended enterprise, thereby encouraging supplier partners to feel like they belong to a larger collective. This is vital if the extended enterprise is going to coordinate effectively and behave like a single firm. Third, I suggested that collaborative advantage does not materialize overnight. Generating value from an extended enterprise takes time, and the orchestrator of the enterprise must patiently put in place, and nurture, value-creation processes. It takes time for the enterprise to evolve to the point where enterprise members have developed strong relationships with each other and have made investments in dedicated assets, set up routines to share knowledge, and built the trust necessary to lower transaction costs within the enterprise. However, once this occurs, the enterprise will be a powerful weapon in the battle for competitive advantage.

Conclusion

A Model for the Future

Virtual integration harnesses the economic benefits of two very different business models; it has the potential to achieve both coordination and focus. If it delivers on that promise, it may well become a new organizational model for the information age.

—Joan Magretta, *Harvard Business Review*

In today's world, it's not the big that eat the small, it's the fast that eat the slow.

—Former Chrysler President Robert Lutz

Future competitive advantage will increasingly be created by teams of companies, rather than by single firms. Single firms will simply be unable to amass the resources and knowledge required to compete with a well-coordinated team of competing companies. The old maxim that "two heads are better than one" is especially applicable in today's business world due to communication technologies that allow for more effective interfirm collaboration. Consequently, competitive advantage will increasingly be jointly created, and shared, by teams of firms within a value chain. Vertical integration will continue to give way to virtual integration. This phenomenon is what I have referred to as collaborative advantage within the extended enterprise.

The winners of the next decade and beyond will understand how to unlock the keys to creating collaborative advantage. They will recognize where and when to make investments in dedicated assets in order to optimize the value chain in which they are embedded. They will develop routines for sharing knowledge with their partners in the extended enterprise, thereby enhancing the competencies of all enterprise members. They will know how to develop trust with those partners so that the extended enterprise can swiftly and flexibly respond to opportunities and threats while maintaining very low transaction costs. And they will also understand that strategy is no longer an individual firm phenomenon but will increasingly be done in concert with a firm's partners in the extended enterprise. Indeed, strategy will be formulated at the extended enterprise level by a group of firms that explicitly take into account the resources and capabilities that reside within the network. This will give them the speed, agility, and resources to respond to opportunities and threats in a way that a single firm cannot. As the Bob Lutz quote at the beginning of the chapter suggests, future competitive advantage will increasingly be based on the speed with which companies can respond to new business opportunities. Perhaps the greatest strength of the extended enterprise is the speed with which a well-coordinated team of companies can mobilize their resources to attack new market opportunities.

While Toyota and Chrysler have been successful with their models of the extended enterprise, new variations of the extended enterprise concept will emerge and flourish. Indeed, I already see the extended enterprise concept being expanded and modified in some important ways.

Future Directions for Toyota and DaimlerChrysler

Thus far, I have described how Toyota and Chrysler have pioneered extended enterprises that have created collaborative advantage. But I am sometimes asked by both executives and academics: "What's next for Toyota and DaimlerChrysler? What are some of the future directions for the extended enterprise?" Although it is difficult to predict exactly how different companies may push the frontier of the extended-enterprise concept, I see at least two initiatives that companies may take to strengthen the power of collaborative advantage. The first is what I refer to as the modular extended enterprise, wherein megasuppliers emerge with primary responsibility for key subsystems in the final product. In this case the final product becomes increasingly modular and the megasuppliers emerge as more equal partners in enterprise activities. The second of these is vertical extension of extended enterprise ideas and concepts through the value chain, beyond just first-tier suppliers.

The Modular Extended Enterprise

A dominant trend in the organization of production (in both the automotive industry and elsewhere) during the past decade has been the shift away from vertical integration as manufacturers have increasingly outsourced parts to their suppliers. Chrysler was the first U.S. automaker to initiate increased outsourcing but has been followed by both Ford and GM, who have spun off their in-house parts divisions Visteon and Delphi, respectively. In chapter 1 I described the trends driving these moves and, more specifically, why a governance profile that is heavy on partnerships is preferred for complex products. A current trend that is hitting the automotive industry (and that often coincides with outsourcing) is *modularization*, a strategy for organizing complex products and processes efficiently. A modular system is composed of subsystems (or modules) that are designed independently but still function as an integrated whole. They can function as a whole because they adhere to visible design rules which specify in detail how the modules will interface, including how they will fit together, connect, and communicate.[1] The computer industry offers an extreme example of modularity, wherein a large number of different companies design their own so-called plug compatible modules—printers, terminals, disk drives, memory, software, even the central-processing units—according to visible design rules. The individual modules are then configured together to create a computer system. This method of organizing has the advantage of allowing the individual companies to design new products with great flexibility (each product/component can have hidden design parameters that do not affect the design beyond the local module) as long as they adhere to the visible design rules. The freedom to experiment with product designs and create entire subassemblies that attach to other subassemblies is what distinguishes modular suppliers from ordinary subcontractors.

Modularization is just beginning to catch on in the automotive industry and is likely to reshape the value chain and influence the future of the extended enterprise. To illustrate, DaimlerChrysler has experimented with assigning responsibility for increasingly large and important subsystems to increasingly large and capable suppliers. For example, rather than worry about designing and managing all of the suppliers that provide inputs to the interior of the car (seats, carpet, fabric, etc.), in some vehicles DaimlerChrysler has given this entire responsibility to Magna International. In fact, Magna and its major competitors, Lear Seating and Johnson Controls, have been buying related suppliers, each attempting to become the worldwide leader in the production of entire car interiors. In similar fashion, Daimler-Chrysler is relying on Dana Corporation to provide a completely built-up rolling chassis for the Dakota pickups its new Brazilian plant will produce. Dana spent $14 million on a plant near the DaimlerChrysler facility to produce the chassis, which accounts for about one-third of the truck's content. DaimlerChrysler Co-Chairman Robert J. Eaton called the plant the automaker's model plant for the future because of its unprecedented use of modular assemblies. Stated Eaton, "In the future, there is going to be no limit to the use of modular assemblies."[2]

Volkswagen has taken this approach even further with its new revolutionary "modular consortium" truck and bus factory in Resende, Brazil. Going beyond traditional outsourcing strategies, VW has outsourced the entire assembly process to eight supplier partners. The supplier partners are: Ichope-Maxion (chassis); Rockwell International (axles and suspension systems); the Remon consortium, a joint venture of Iochpe-Maxion, Bridgestone, and Borlem SA (wheels and tires); Cummins Engine Co. Inc. and Germany's Motoren Werke Mannheim AG (engines/powertrain); VDO Kinzie Comercio e Servicos (interior/upholstery); Delga Automotiva Industria e Commercio (cabin frame); and Eisenmann GmbH (painting). Another partner, Union Mantein, is in charge of the internal flow of materials and assembly-line supplies. VW handles only the final production module, which is final product testing. Each partner occupies a section of the plant, which has seven sets of yellow stripes that divide it into seven "mini-factories." The suppliers are responsible for assembling their module in their mini-factory. Once a supplier assembles a module, it is moved to the final assembly line, which runs right next to the line of mini-factories. But the only feature that delineates the suppliers' mini-factory from VW's assembly line is a yellow line painted on the floor. Once a module crosses the yellow line it becomes VW's responsibility. Even so, it is the supplier's employees who move it across the line and attach it to the vehicle. VW only has a single employee involved in final car assembly, a master who oversees the final assembly process to ensure the modules are attached properly and to do a final quality test.[3]

Naturally, a key challenge is the systemic integration of the activities of the partners. The partners have their own office space within the plant which facilitates intense, face-to-face communication. All partners meet early every morning to review the day's production schedule and consult with each other on technical problems. The plant's 52 networked information systems provide immediate access to data stored electronically. Everyone in the plant wears the same style uniform, which features a VW logo on the upper left pocket and the specific partner's logo on the right.[4]

The plant and vehicle output are clearly owned and controlled by both VW and its supplier partners. While VW invested some $250 million to provide the basic plant infrastructure, the supplier partners contributed an additional $50 million to the plant. The partners have guaranteed fixed-term contracts that span from 5 to 15 years (escape clauses in the contracts allow VW to replace a supplier for poor performance). Supplier partners are paid on a per-vehicle basis and no supplier is paid until the vehicle clears final inspection—not when parts are delivered, as is the usual custom in the industry. Thus, for payment purposes, all suppliers are accountable for total quality and vehicle sales in the marketplace.[5] Risks and rewards are truly shared by VW and the supplier partners in its Resende extended enterprise.

So far, the experiment seems to be working. VW substantially reduced its up-front investment costs, and instead of negotiating with over 400 suppliers (as it does in its other truck and bus plants) it only negotiates with 8 suppliers. But more importantly, the modular extended enterprise arrangement allows VW to respond quickly to market demands. In Brazil, the truck and bus market is very demanding, with individual customers wanting to apply a personal touch. In the past, accommodating such requests would take months for VW to get agreement from all suppliers. Now they get together immediately and make decisions on the spot. Moreover, it is estimated that vehicles will cost 15–25 percent less at the Resende plant and "the 'pre-delivery' functional audit has already shown remarkable improvement in bus-chassis quality."[6] This is only possible because of more effective collaboration. States plant manager Roberto Barretti: "We have no fences between VW and the partners. We try to do everything together." Moreover, Barretti claims that "this system is possible for any product built on an assembly line. It could be a car, a refrigerator or a TV."[7]

It is worth noting that Toyota is taking a very cautious approach to modularization, because with a modular approach it is difficult to achieve the high level of product integrity and fit that Toyota demands in its vehicles (most of us have experienced the frustrations of modular designs with our plug-compatible computer systems that often do not work well together; these compatibility problems are much more severe in a complex system like an automobile). Naturally, solving the coordination and integration problems (creating the appropriate visible design rules) among the mega suppliers will be a key challenge. But the automaker that is able to effectively integrate a modular approach with its partner suppliers and achieve the quality that customers demand will realize key advantages in cost and speed to market.

In summary, in the future extended enterprise automakers will do even less design and production than they do today. Instead, they will focus their resources and competencies on vehicle design and styling, branding (sales and marketing), systems integration (integrating all of the vehicle modules and setting the visible design rules), and knowledge management (sharing best practices within the enterprise with regard to design, manufacturing, etc.). Rather than work with hundreds of suppliers as they do now, they will work largely with a dozen or so megasuppliers who provide the entire car interior, the powertrain, the chassis, the cabin frame, the instrument panel, and so forth. This process will likely shift some power to key suppliers who will control the key modules, thereby making the automaker even more interdependent with the key members of its extended enterprise. Getting these suppliers to work as a team will be a critical challenge for the automaker. These megasuppliers will become more equal partners in the product-development and production process and will have complete responsibility for a major subsystem. This may include becoming an equity partner in the final product as well as being assigned responsibility to "wheel in" their subsystem and oversee final assembly of their subsystem in the car assembly plant. However, I should note that these so-called megasuppliers need not, and probably should not, be fully integrated into all related components. Integrating into all component areas will expose them to the liabilities of vertical integration (described in chapter 2) and make them vulnerable in the event of an economic downturn. They may be better off coordinating the efforts of a network of suppliers with whom they create collaborative advantage in their own extended companies.

Vertical Extension of the Enterprise

Virtually all of the discussion so far has focused on Toyota's and Chrysler's attempts to create advantages by working in collaborative fashion with its first-tier suppliers only. However, it is important to recognize that tier-1 suppliers also outsource a large percentage of their inputs to tier-2 suppliers, and so on. Thus, if Toyota wants its extended enterprise to be able to quickly respond to strategic threats or opportunities, it must be able to mobilize the resources of suppliers beyond just the first tier. To illustrate, in the late 1970s and early 1980s Toyota worked very hard to improve the quality of its vehicles due to perceived lower quality relative to its U.S. and German competitors. Toyota executives recall that during that time period, quality issues were paramount within its supplier association activities, its consulting activities, and its *jishuken* activities. But these activities only involved its tier-1 suppliers. For Toyota to improve its quality more rapidly, its tier-2 and tier-3 suppliers also needed to improve quality. Toyota has more than 5,000 tier-2 suppliers and more than 40,000 tier-3 suppliers in Japan.[8] Toyota does not possibly have the resources to individually help all of those suppliers improve quality. However, if each tier-1 supplier replicates Toyota's knowledge-sharing processes with its suppliers, then valuable knowledge with regard to quality can be quickly diffused throughout the value chain.

To illustrate, Denso, Toyota's largest supplier, has replicated Toyota's supplier association concept with its suppliers. Indeed, Denso's supplier association is almost identical to Toyota's in its structure and objectives. Denso's association has both general meetings and committees on cost, quality, safety, and management (many tier-2 suppliers are relatively unsophisticated; thus, Denso's association provides management training). Not surprisingly, since more than 50 percent of Denso's sales go to Toyota, the focus of its association's activities typically reflects Toyota's objectives. As one Denso executive explained: "Our association is completely independent from Toyota's. But the focus of our activities and initiatives is similar because Toyota is such an important customer. . . .Also, it's a way for us to pass on what we've learned from participating in *kyohokai* [Toyota's association]."[9] Thus, the Denso supplier association becomes a vertical extension of Toyota's, thereby encouraging both tier-1 and tier-2 suppliers to quickly respond to Toyota's strategic objectives.

Unlike Toyota's association, which offers membership to all tier-1 suppliers, not all of Denso's suppliers are allowed to join its supplier association. Instead, due to limited resources and a large number of suppliers that provide low-value inputs, only those suppliers who meet specific size, dependency, and performance criteria are allowed to join (i.e., suppliers must sell at least $10 million per year to Denso or have 30 percent of their total sales to Denso). Consequently, Denso focuses its assistance on the 69 largest suppliers that comprise its supplier association. Naturally, these suppliers are also the most important tier-2 contributors to Toyota's extended enterprise. Thus, by replicating this pattern down through its supply chain, Denso helps Toyota achieve its strategic objectives.

Denso is not alone in replicating Toyota's practices with its suppliers. Indeed, by 1995 approximately 79 percent of Toyota's tier-1 suppliers had established their own supplier associations, thus beginning the vertical extension of collaborative advantage concepts throughout the entire value chain. As a result of this vertical extension of extended enterprise practices, Toyota's entire production network is better able to communicate, share knowledge, and collaborate to achieve common objectives.

We are just starting to see a similar vertical extension of extended enterprise ideas within DaimlerChrysler's network. For example, some tier-1 suppliers are starting to implement their own version of DaimlerChrysler's SCORE program. ITT Automotive is among a small handful of suppliers that have implemented a version of the SCORE program with their suppliers. Although in the early stages, ITT Automotive reports promising results. Not surprisingly, some of the value-creation ideas that tier-2 suppliers generate require DaimlerChrysler's involvement and approval—or, in effect, feed right into Daimler-Chrysler's SCORE program. This enhances knowledge sharing across a larger group of firms who are trying to collaborate to create quality vehicles as quickly and inexpensively as possible. Thus, Daimler-Chrysler benefits from the vertical extension of its SCORE program. DaimlerChrysler recognizes this fact and gives awards to suppliers that have become "role models in the supplier community for Extended Enterprise initiatives."[10] ITT Automotive was chosen as a recipient of this award by engaging in a number of supplier development initiatives, including "conducting annual key supplier conferences to strengthen the communication channels in the extended enterprise, the implementation of a worldwide supplier quality rating system to ensure that only the best global suppliers are selected, and the development of a proactive supplier cost reduction program (e.g., SCORE) to encourage the use of continuous improvement initiatives throughout the supply chain."[11] TRW implemented its version of a SCORE program (called Success) with its suppliers, and in the first five months generated $6.2 million in savings.

In summary, the vertical diffusion of extended enterprise concepts will allow Toyota and DaimlerChrysler to respond even more quickly to opportunities and threats because their supply chains will be even more flexible, responsive, and capable. Of course, this assumes that both companies will be able to continue to innovate with regard to creating collaborative advantage with its suppliers. I have every confidence that Toyota will continue to develop new avenues for advantage in its extended enterprise. But my follow-up research suggests that this will be a key challenge for DaimlerChrysler.

The Future of DaimlerChrysler's Extended Enterprise

Daimler is now in the process of becoming familiar with Chrysler's extended enterprise philosophy. According to DaimlerChrysler's Jeff Trimmer, head of procurement strategy: "We have agreed that we are going to accept the 'extended enterprise' philosophy, but we haven't yet agreed on the processes. Our approach right now is to take it slow and just see what we can learn from each other."[12] Right now both Chrysler and Daimler are managing their suppliers in nearly the same way as they were before the merger. But different corporate cultures, different supplier management strategies, and different sources of advantage in the marketplace may make it difficult for the new DaimlerChrysler to fully adopt Chrysler's extended enterprise practices. Let me explain why.

It is no surprise that America's Chrysler and Germany's Daimler-Benz have different corporate cultures that are reflective of their native cultures. A senior DaimlerChrysler executive described these cultural differences with the following analogy.

> Our different approaches to problem solving are illustrated by how we would each respond to opening a new board game. The Americans at Chrysler would open the game and while someone started reading through the instructions the others would set up the board and the game pieces. After getting about halfway through the instructions the group, eager to get started, would decide to start play and then figure out the game as they went along. In contrast, the Germans at Daimler would open the game, and before setting up the board they would carefully read all of the instructions, at least once. Then, after running some game simulations for a couple of days, they would be ready to start play.[13]

This illustration contrasts Daimler's obsession for detail and up-front planning with Chrysler's desire to jump into a problem and figure it out as they go along. These different approaches may make it difficult for DaimlerChrysler to continue to innovate with regard to the extended enterprise concept.

First, Daimler's organization has not been designed to be responsive to suppliers in the same way that Chrysler's has been. For example, Daimler's version of Chrysler's SCORE (cost reduction) program, called TANDEM, has been relatively unsuccessful at producing suggestions from suppliers. States one DaimlerChrysler (former Chrysler) executive, "They [Daimler] have a suggestion program like SCORE, but the box is usually empty." Why? One reason is that Chrysler encourages suppliers to constantly submit cost-reduction ideas, and it has developed a process for quick evaluation, approval, and implementation. Chrysler gives SCORE targets both to its internal engineers and buyers as well as to its suppliers. As a result, suppliers are motivated to offer suggestions, and each Chrysler vehicle is constantly changing in subtle ways that lower costs and increase profits for both Chrysler and its suppliers. By comparison, Daimler is much more cautious about allowing changes to its vehicles and has typically only allowed changes to its vehicles once each year (this should not be a surprise because Daimler competes on quality at the high end of the market and, consequently, is very cautious about allowing changes to its vehicles without considerable testing). As a result, Daimler's suppliers have not developed the processes or a culture of constantly searching for opportunities to reduce the cost of the parts they produce. Thus, fewer suggestions are offered and fewer are approved. Not surprisingly, Daimler and its suppliers expect to make fewer changes to a vehicle after volume production, in part because they do more effective up-front planning.

Second, Chrysler simply expects more engineering from its suppliers and has shifted more responsibility to suppliers than has Daimler. Daimler possesses strong engineering skills, which it uses to a greater degree in the overall design and development of a vehicle. Daimler wins in the marketplace by designing a high-end vehicle that demands design elegance. Consequently, it is less likely to relinquish full responsibility for major components and sub-systems to its suppliers. Thus, as an organization Daimler views itself as less reliant on its suppliers for its success.

These differences could create substantial obstacles to implementing the extended enterprise philosophy and processes within the new DaimlerChrysler. Daimler executives may point to the fact that "we're different" and argue that the extended enterprise concepts are not applicable. Doing so would be a mistake. Daimler need only look at Toyota's Lexus division to see that extended enterprise ideas can work very well in the development and production of high-end vehicles. Only time will tell whether or not the combined entity will continue to generate the performance advantages enjoyed by Chrysler during the 1990s. Even the departed Tom Stallkamp, who left DaimlerChrysler largely due to differences in philosophy, concedes that "whether DaimlerChrysler can succeed with the extended enterprise is an open issue. They have a tremendous opportunity. But it won't work if Daimler wants to dominate and control the supply chain."[14] One thing seems clear. If the new DaimlerChrysler hopes to continue to create collaborative advantages, all of DaimlerChrysler's executives will have to fully embrace the new mindset required by the extended enterprise philosophy.

Some Final Thoughts Regarding Collaborative Advantage

If future competitive advantage will increasingly be created by teams of companies, then future executives will have to change their perspective on how to maximize their company's profits. In fact, a fundamental change in mindset is required. The traditional executive perspective (shown in Figure Concl.1) has been to focus on the individual firm's economics and to create competitive advantage through physical, technological, and financial assets that can be leveraged to appropriate as much of the value chain's profits as possible. Thus, the perspective is self-focused, based on strong boundaries of the firm, and dedicated to achieving relative bargaining power. Firms in the value chain view the size of the "pie" as relatively fixed, and, consequently, their dealings with other firms reflect a zero-sum game mentality (see Figure Concl.2).

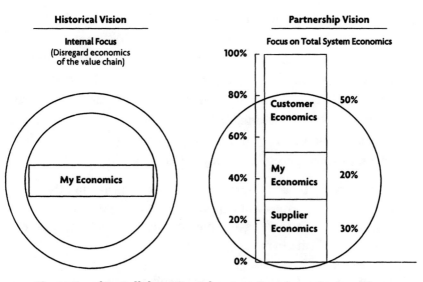

Figure Concl.1. Collaborative Advantage Requires a System View

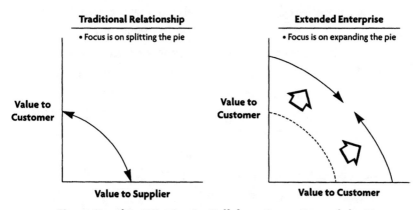

Figure Concl.2. Winning By Collaborating to Expand the Pie

In contrast, achieving collaborative advantage requires a focus on the economics of the entire value chain, or extended enterprise. Rather than maintaining a bargaining orientation, the firms in the enterprise focus their energies and resources on how they can optimize the performance of the entire system. In short, rather than focusing their energies on splitting the pie, they focus their energies on expanding the size of the pie, so that all parties are better off regardless of their percentage share. This new mindset will often lead to different firm strategies and different firm behavior. Let me offer a brief illustration of how this new perspective may prompt executives to choose strategies that contradict those recommended by previous strategy paradigms.

In Michael Porter's seminal book *Competitive Strategy*, he argued that firms should be eager to increase the number of their suppliers, thereby maximizing bargaining power and profits.

> In purchasing, then, the goal is to find mechanisms to offset or surmount these sources of suppliers' power.... Purchases of an item can be spread among alternate suppliers in such a way as to improve the firm's bargaining power.[15]

This strategy is in direct contrast to the collaborative advantage perspective offered in this book. According to the collaborative advantage perspective, firms can increase profits by increasing their dependence on a smaller number of suppliers, thereby increasing the incentives of suppliers to share knowledge and make performance-enhancing investments in dedicated assets. By committing to a small number of suppliers, the buyer firm can guarantee them greater bargaining power (in the future). The fact that the supplier can now claim a greater percentage of jointly generated (future) profits gives them greater incentives to make non-contractible investments, such as investments in innovation, responsiveness, and information sharing. In the end, the buyer ends up being better off by keeping a smaller piece of a bigger pie.

During my extensive research of the automobile industry, I have come to the conclusion that this logic explains much of Chrysler's collaborate advantage over General Motors. I am convinced that General Motors, due to its emphasis on negotiation skills and bargaining power, extracts a greater percentage of the pie that it jointly creates with suppliers relative to Chrysler. However, Chrysler wins by keeping a smaller piece of a bigger pie. Because Chrysler is a more attractive and more profitable customer for suppliers, more resources and information flow in Chrysler's direction. As a supplier, if I have additional resources (an incremental unit of engineering resources) I am more likely to put those resources to work for Chrysler to generate SCORE ideas (from which I can appropriate greater profits) than for General Motors. Chrysler has become the preferred customer and is the preferred extended enterprise. Thus, suppliers have greater incentives to make sure that Chrysler's extended enterprise is successful. Of course, this is somewhat risky for Chrysler, which must continue to trust that its suppliers will identify with and contribute to Chrysler's extended enterprise in ways not specifically dictated in a legal contract. But so far Chrysler has not been disappointed. And Toyota's history of creating collaborative advantages, and maintaining them, is even longer than Chrysler's. The power of effective interfirm teamwork is phenomenal and often underestimated.

As Chrysler and Toyota have both demonstrated, the rewards of this approach can be enormous. Let me remind the reader that Toyota has been the most profitable automaker over the past two decades and Chrysler has achieved profit performance never before seen in the history of the U.S. industry (at least during the 25 years that profit per vehicle information has been tracked). Creating an extended enterprise requires new behavior, new processes, new routines—most of which must recognize a firm's *interdependence* on other firms for its success. Naturally, this does not come without risks. But as one executive once reminded me, "the definition of insanity is someone who continues to do things the same way and expects improved results."[16] For executives who desire improved results, the extended enterprise is the wave of the future.

Notes

Preface

1. See Dyer, J.H., W.G. Ouchi (1993) "Japanese Style Partnerships: Giving Companies a Competitive Edge." *Sloan Management Review*, 35, no. 1, 51–63.

Introduction

Epigraph Source: Magretta, J. (1998) "The power of virtual integration: An interview with Dell Computer's Michael Dell." *Harvard Business Review*, (March–April): 75.

1. Porter, M.E. (1980). *Competitive Strategy*. New York: The Free Press.

2. Rumelt, R.P. (1984). "Towards a Strategic Theory of the Firm." In R.B. Lamb, ed., *Competitive Strategic Management*. Englewood Cliffs, N.J.: Prentice-Hall, pp. 556–571; Wernerfelt, B. (1984). "A Resource-Based View of the Firm." *Strategic Management Journal* 5: 171–180; Barney, J.B. (1991). "Firm Resources and Sustained Competitive Advantage." *Journal of Management* 17: 99–120.

3. Rumelt, "Towards a Strategic Theory of the Firm,"; Barney, "Firm Resources and Sustained Competitive Advantage"; Dierickx, I., & K. Cool (1989). "Asset Stock Accumulation and Sustainability of Competitive Advantage." *Management Science* 35, no. 12: 1504–1513.

4. Von Hippel, E. (1988). *The Sources of Innovation*. New York: Oxford University Press; Stalk, G., & T.M. Hout (1990). *Competing Against Time*. New York: The Free Press.

5. Ministry of International Trade and Industry (1987). *White Paper on Small and Medium Enterprises in Japan*. Tokyo: MITI, pp. 36–37.

6. Data on increased outsourcing can be found in Bresnen, M., & C. Fowler (1994). "The Organizational Correlates and Consequences of Subcontracting:

Evidence from a Survey Of South Wales Businesses." *Journal of Management Studies* 31, no. 6: 847–864; Nishiguchi, T. (1994). *Strategic Industrial Sourcing.* New York: Oxford University Press.

7. Nishiguchi, *Strategic Industrial Sourcing*; Dyer, J. H., & H. Singh (1998). "The Relational View: Cooperative Strategy and Sources of Interorganizational Competitive Advantage." *Academy of Management Review* 23, no. 4: 660–679.

8. Benjamin Gomes-Casseres makes this same argument in *The Alliance Revolution*. Cambridge, Mass.: Harvard University Press.

9. Evans, P.E. and T.S. Wurster (2000). *Blown to Bits.* Boston: Harvard University Business School Press.

10. Dyer, J.H., & W.G. Ouchi (1993). "Japanese Style Business Partnerships: Giving Companies a Competitive Edge." *Sloan Management Review* 35, no. 1: 51–63.

11. Author interview, October 28, 1999.

12. Dore, R. (1983). "Goodwill and the Spirit of Market Capitalism." *British Journal of Sociology* 34, no. 4; Gerlach, M.L. (1992). *Alliance Capitalism.* Berkeley: University of California Press; Womack, J.P., D.T. Jones, & D. Roos (1990). *The Machine That Changed the World.* New York: Harper Perennial; Clark, K.B., & T. Fujimoto (1991). *Product Development Performance.* Boston: Harvard Business School Press; Nishiguchi, *Strategic Industrial Sourcing.*

13. Lieberman, M. (1994). "The Diffusion of 'Lean Manufacturing' in the Japanese and U.S." Change Conference, Shizuoka, Japan, August 28–30.

14. Author interview, November 1992.

15. Womack, Jones, & Roos, *The Machine That Changed the World.*

16. Author interview, November 1995.

17. Womack, J.P., & D.T. Jones (1994). "From Lean Production to the Lean Enterprise," *Harvard Business Review* (March-April): 96.

18. "Toyota Set to Join Online Trade Exchange." *Financial Times,* March 10, 2000, A1.

19. Author Interview, March 6, 2000.

20. Nishiguchi, *Strategic Industrial Sourcing*; Lieberman, "The Diffusion of 'Lean Manufacturing"; Dyer, J.H. (1996). "Specialized Supplier Networks as a Source of Competitive Advantage: Evidence from the Auto Industry," *Strategic Management Journal* 17, no. 4: 271–292.

21. Byrne, J.A. (1993). "The Virtual Corporation," *Business Week* (February 8): 98–102.

22. Drucker, Peter (1946). *The Concept of the Corporation.* New York: John Day.

23. I adopt the definition of a complex-product industry offered by Clark and Fujimoto, in *Product Development Performance*, pp. 9–12.

24. For a description of three different types of interdependence, see Thompson, J.D. (1967). *Organizations in Action.* New York: McGraw-Hill. Reciprocal interdependence is the most complex and requires the greatest amount of coordination.

25. *Fortune* (January 11, 1999): 93.

26. *The Economist* (May 9, 1998): 62.

27. *The Economist* (May 9, 1998): 61–61.

28. *Wards Auto World* 34, no. 6 (1998): 5–15.

29. *The Economist* (May 9, 1998): 61–62.

Chapter 1

Epigraph Source: Fine, C.H. (1998). *Clockspeed.* Reading: Perseus Books.

1. Anand, B., & T. Khanna (1999). "Do Firms Learn to Create Value? The Case of Alliances." *Strategic Management Journal,* special issue, conference on strategic networks.

2. Clemons, E.K., S.P. Reddi & M.C. Row (1993). "The Impact of Information Technology on the Organization of Economic Activity: The 'Move to the Middle' Hypothesis." *Journal of Management Information Systems* 10, no. 2: 9–35.

3. Tully, S. (1993). "The Modular Corporation." *Fortune* (February 8): 106.

4. Dell, M. (1999) "The Virtual Firm." The World in 1999, The Economist Publications, p. 96.

5. Dyer, J. H., & W.G. Ouchi (1993). "Japanese Style Business Partnerships: Giving Companies a Competitive Edge." *Sloan Management Review* 35, no. 1: 51–63.

6. Author interview, December 1, 1995.

7. Dyer, & Ouchi, "Japanese Style Business Partnerships." McMillan, J. (1990). "Managing Suppliers: Incentive Systems in Japanese and U.S. Industry." *California Management Review* (Summer): 38–55.

8. Enright, M. (1991). *Japanese Facsimilie Industry.* Boston: Harvard Business School Press.

9. Clemons, Reddi, & Row, "The Impact of Information Technology"; "One world?" (1997) *The Economist* (October 18): 79.

10. Badaracco, Jr. J.L. (1991). *The Knowledge Link.* Boston: Harvard Business School Press.

11. Butler, P., T.W. Hall, A.M. Hanna, L. Mendonca, B. Auguste, J. Manyika, A. Sahay (1997). "A Revolution in Interaction." *McKinsey Quarterly,* no. 1: 4–23.

12. Pine, J. (1993). *Mass Customization.* Cambridge, Mass.: Harvard University Press.

13. "Driving Detroit to Tiers." *The Alliance Analyst,* (September 14, 1994): 1–4.

14. Walton, M. (1997). *Car: A Drama of the American Workplace.* New York: W.W. Norton & Company.

15. Abegglen, J.C., & G. Stalk, Jr. (1985). *Kaisha: The Japanese Corporation.* Basic Books; Kotler, P., L. Fahey, & S. Jatusripitak (1985). *The New Competition.* Englewood Cliffs, N.J.: Prentice-Hall.

16. Jorgenson, D.W., M. Kuroda, & M. Nishimizu (1987). "Japan-U.S. Industry

Level Productivity Comparisons, 1960–1979." *Journal of the Japanese and International Economies* 1: 1–30.

17. Ministry of International Trade and Industry (1987). *White Paper on Small and Medium Enterprises in Japan*, Tokyo: MITI, pp. 36–37.

18. Smitka, M.J. (1991). *Competitive Ties: Subcontracting in the Japanese Automotive Industry*. New York: Columbia University Press.

19. Gerlach, M.L. (1992). *Alliance Capitalism*. Berkeley: University of California Press.

20. Sako, M. (1992). *Prices, Quality, and Trust*. Cambridge: Cambridge University Press.

21. Williamson, O.E. (1985). *The Economic Institutions of Capitalism*. New York: The Free Press.

Chapter 2

Epigraph sources: Author interview, June 10, 1996; Jacobson, G., & J. Hillkirk (1987). *Xerox: American Samurai*. New York: Collier Books, p. 109.

1. Kenny, M., & R. Florida (1993). *Beyond Mass Production*. New York: Oxford University Press.

2. Ibid., p. 146.

3. Author Interview, June 1992.

4. *Fortune* (March 29, 1999): 144C.

5. Anderson, J.C., M. Rungtasanatham & R.G. Schroedere (1994). "A Theory of Quality Management Underlying the Deming Management Method." *Academy of Management Review* 19 no. 3: 472–509. Deming, W.E. (1986). *Out of the Crises*. Cambridge: M.I.T. Press.

6. Juran, J.A.M. (1989). *Juran on Leadership for Quality*. New York: Free Press.

7. Nishiguchi, T. (1994). *Strategic Industrial Sourcing*. New York: Oxford University Press; Clark, K.B., & T. Fujimoto (1991). *Product Development Performance*. Boston: Harvard Business School Press.

8. Stalk, G., & T.M. Hout. (1990). *Competing Against Time*. New York: The Free Press.

9. Clark & Fujimoto, *Product Development Performance*.

10. Stalk & Hout, *Competing Against Time*; Clark & Fujimoto, *Product Development Performance*.

11. Nobeoka, K. (1993). "Multi-Project Management: Strategy and Organization in Automobile Product Development." M.I.T., Ph.D. dissertation.

12. Clark & Fujimoto. *Product Development Performance*

13. Wu, Y.C. & J. Liker (1999). "Customer Policies and Lean Supply Chain Management: Comparing U.S. and Japanese Automakers in North America." University of Michigan Working Paper.

14. Williamson, O.E. (1985). *The Economic Institutions of Capitalism*. New York: The Free Press.

15. Porter, M. (1985). *Competitive Advantage*. New York: The Free Press.

16. McMillan, 1990; Dyer, J.H., & W.G. Ouchi (1993). "Japanese Style Business Partnerships: Giving Companies a Competitive Edge." *Sloan Management Review* 35, no. 1: 51–63.

17. Von Hippel, E. (1988). *The Sources of Innovation*. New York: Oxford University Press; Harrigan, K. (1985). *Strategic Flexibility*. Lexington, Mass.: Lexington Books.

18. Collis, D. (1992). "The Automotive Component Group at GM." Boston: Harvard Business School Press.

19. Harrigan, K. *Strategic Flexibility*.

20. Collis, "The Automotive Component Group at GM."

21. Ibid., p. 13.

22. Antle, R., & A. Smith (1986). "An Empirical Investigation of the Relative Performance Evaluation of Corporate Executives." *Journal of Accounting Research* 24, (spring): 1–32; Ehrenberg, R.G., & G.T. Milkovich (1987). "Compensation and Firm Performance." In *Human Resources and the Performance of the Firm*, ed. Kleiner, et al. Industrial Relations Research Association Series.

23. Salinger, M.A. (1984). "Tobins q, Unionization, and the Concentration-Profits Relationship." *Rand Journal* 14: 159–70.

24. Internal study at U.S. automaker, 1990.

25. Smitka, M.J. (1991). *Competitive Ties: Subcontracting in the Japanese Automotive Industry*. New York: Columbia University Press.

26. Saxenian, A. (1990). "Regional Networks and the Resurgence of Silicon Valley." *California Management Review* (fall): 89–112.

27. Saxenian, A. (1991). "The Origins and Dynamics of Production Networks in Silicon Valley." *Research Policy* 10: 423–37.

28. See Bartmess, A., & K. Cerny. (1993). "Building Competitive Advantage through a Global Network of Capabilities." *California Management Review* 35, no. 2: 2–27.

Chapter 3

Epigraph source: Author interview, June 10, 1996.

1. Evans, P. and T.S. Wurster (2000). *Blown to Bits*. Boston: Harvard University Business School Press.

2. Nishiguchi, T. (1994). *Strategic Industrial Sourcing*. New York: Oxford University Press; Lieberman, M. (1994). "The Diffusion of 'Lean Manufacturing' in the Japanese and U.S. Change." Conference, Shizuoka, Japan, August 28–30.

3. Lieberman, M. (1994). "The Diffusion of 'Lean Manufacturing.'"

4. Lieberman's analysis on inventory reductions over time mirrors the labor productivity data. Moreover, Mari Sako (1997) replicated Lieberman's study in

the United Kingdom with virtually identical results; presentation at the International Motor Vehicle Program Conference in Kyung Ju, Korea.

5. Kogut, B., & U. Zander (1992). "Knowledge of the Firm, Combinative Capabilities, and the Replication of Technology." *Organization Science* 3, no. 3: 383–397; Grant, R. (1996). "Prospering in Dynamically-Competitive Environments: Organizational Capability as Knowledge Integration." *Organization Science* 7, no. 4: 375–387; Ryle, G. (1984). *The Concept of Mind.* Chicago: University of Chicago Press, pp. 29–34.

6. Nelson, R., & S. Winter (1982). *An Evolutionary Theory of Economic Change.* Cambridge, Mass.: Belknap Press; Kogut & Zander, "Knowledge of the Firm"; Szulanski, G. (1996). "Exploring Internal Stickiness: Impediments to the Transfer of Best Practice Within the Firm." *Strategic Management Journal* 17: 27–43.

7. Nonaka, I., & H. Takeuchi (1995). *The Knowledge Creating Company.* New York: Oxford University Press.

8. Internal Toyota document, 1996.

9. Author interview, November 17, 1997.

10. Internal Toyota document, 1995.

11. Author interview, February 1998.

12. Author interview, November 1996.

13. Author interview, November 1996.

14. Author interview, November 1996.

15. Author interview, February 1998.

16. Author interview, November 1996.

17. Author interview, November 1997.

18. Author interview, November 1966.

19. Lincoln, J.R., M. Gerlach, & P. Takahashi (1992). "*Keiretsu* Networks in the Japanese Economy: A Dyad Analysis of Intercorporate Ties." *American Sociological Review* 57: 361–585; Gerlach, M.L. (1992). *Alliance Capitalism.* Berkeley: University of California Press.

20. Author interview, June 10, 1997.

21. Notes taken from a working paper by Kenji Wada.

22. Author interview, September 1993.

23. Porter, M. (1980). *Competitive Strategy.* New York: The Free Press.

24. Author interview, June 6, 1997.

25. Author interview, September 5, 1997.

26. Author interview, November 19, 1996.

27. Wu, Y.C. & J. Liker (1999). "Customer Policies and Lean Supply Chain Management: Comparing U.S. and Japanese Automakers in North America." University of Michigan Working Paper.

28. Author interview, February 25, 1998.

29. *Automotive Industries* (April 13, 1996); Dyer, J.H. (1996). "Specialized Supplier Networks as a Source of Competitive Advantage: Evidence from the Auto Industry." *Strategic Management Journal* 17, no. 4: 271–292.

Chapter 4

Epigraph sources: Butler, P.T.W. Hall, A.M. Hanna, L. Mendonca, B. Auguste, J. Manyika, & A. Sahay (1997). "A Revolution in Interaction." *McKinsey Quarterly*, no. 1: 5; Author interview, October 25, 1995.

1. Dore, R. (1983). "Goodwill and the Spirit of Market Capitalism." *British Journal of Sociology* 34, no. 4; Sako, M. (1991). "The Role of 'Trust' in Japanese Buyer-Supplier Relationships." *Ricerche Economich* 45, nos. 2–3: 449–474; Gulati, R. (1995). "Familiarity Breeds Trust? The Implications of Repeated Ties for Contractual Choice in Alliances." *Academy of Management Journal* 38: 85–112; Barney, J.B., & M.H. Hansen (1994). "Trustworthiness as a Source of Competitive Advantage." *Strategic Management Journal* 15: 175–190.

2. Aoki, M. (1998). *Information, Incentives, and Bargaining in the Japanese Economy*. New York: Cambridge University Press; Clark, K.B., & T. Fujimoto (1991). *Product Development Performance*. Boston: Harvard Business School Press; Nishiguchi, T. (1994). *Strategic Industrial Sourcing*. New York: Oxford University Press.

3. Asanuma, B. (1989). "Manufacturer-Supplier Relationships in Japan and the Concept of Relation-Specific Skill." *Journal of the Japanese and International Economies* 3: 1–30; Lorenz, E.H. (1988). "Neither Friends nor Strangers: Informal Networks of Subcontracting in French Industry." In *Trust: Making and Breaking Cooperative Relations*, ed. D. Gambetta, New York: Blackwell, pp. 194–210; Dyer, J.H. (1996). "Specialized Supplier Networks as a Source of Competitive Advantage: Evidence from the Auto Industry," *Strategic Management Journal* 17, no. 4: 271–292.

4. Dore, "Goodwill and the Spirit of Market Capitalism"; Ring, P.S., & A.H. Van de Ven (1992). "Structuring Cooperative Relationships Between Organizations." *Strategic Management Journal* 13: 483–498; Sabel, C. (1993). "Studied Trust: Building New Form of Cooperation in a Volatile Economy." *Human Relations*, 46 no. 9: 1133–1170; Barney & Hansen, "Trustworthiness as a Source of Competitive Advantage."

5. Zaheer, A., B. McEvily, & V. Perrone (1998). "Does Trust Matter? Exploring the Effects of Interorganizational and Interpersonal Trust on Performance." *Organization Science* 9, no. 2: 141–159.

6. Deutsch, M. (1958). "Trust and Suspicion." *Journal of Conflict Resolution* 2: 265–279; Mayer, R.C., J.H. Davis, & F.D. Schoorman (1995). "An Integrative Model of Organizational Trust." *Academy of Management Review* 20, no. 3: 709–734.

7. Nishiguchi, T. (1994). *Strategic Industrial Sourcing*. New York: Oxford University Press; Dyer, "Specialized Supplier Networks."

8. Pine II, B.J. (1993). *Mass Customization*. Cambridge, Mass.: Harvard University Press.

9. Lorenz, "Neither Friends nor Strangers"; Aoki, *Information, Incentives, and Bargaining in the Japanese Economy*.

10. See North, D.C. (1990). *Institutions, Institutional Change, and Economic Performance.* Cambridge, UK: Cambridge University Press.

11. Ibid., p. 7.

12. Williamson, O.E. (1985). *The Economic Institutions of Capitalism.* New York: The Free Press; Hennart, J. (1993). "Explaining the Swollen Middle: Why Most Transactions are a Mix of 'Market' and 'Hierarchy,' " *Organization Science* 4, no. 4: 529–547; North, *Institutions, Institutional Change and Economic Performance.*

13. Uzzi, B. (1997). "Social Structure and Competition in Interfirm Networks: The Paradox of Embeddedness." *Administrative Science Quarterly* 42: 35–67.

14. Gulati, R. (1995). "Familiarity Breeds Trust?"; Larson, A. (1992). "Network Dyads in Entrepreneurial Settings: A Study of the Governance of Exchange Relationships," *Administrative Science Quarterly* 37: 76–104.

15. Author interview, September 25, 1994.

16. The pearson correlation between the automaker's procurement costs and the percentage of time spent on bargaining and assigning blame for problems was very high at r = .60.

17. The pearson correlation between the automaker's trustworthiness score and its procurement costs was very high at r = .66.

18. Author interview, April 1993.

19. Author interview, September 25 1994.

20. Author interview, October 1993.

21. Author interview, June 1996.

22. Asanuma, "Manufacturer-Supplier Relationships in Japan"; Parkhe, (1993). "Strategic Alliance Structuring: A Game Theoretic and Transaction Cost Examination of Interfirm Cooperation." *The Academy of Management Journal* 36, no. 4: 794–829; Dyer, J.H. (1996). "Specialized Supplier Networks."

23. Klein, B., R.G. Crawford, & A.A. Alchian (1978). "Vertical Integration, Appropriable Rents, and the Competitive Contracting Process." *Journal of Law and Economics* 21: 297, 326.

24. See Dyer, J.H. (1997) "Effective Interfirm Collaboration: How Firms Minimize Transaction Costs and Maximize Transaction Value." *Strategic Management Journal* 18, no. 7: 535–556; Lyons, B.R. (1994). "Contracts and Specific Investment: An Empirical Test of Transaction Cost Theory." *Journal of Economics and Management Strategy* 3, no. 2: 257–278.

25. Lyons, "Contracts and Specific Investment."

26. Author interview, September 12, 1992.

27. Author interview, September 11, 1992.

28. Butler, J.K. (1991). "Toward Understanding and Measuring Conditions of Trust: Evolution of a Conditions of Trust Inventory." *Journal of Management* 17: 643–663; Heide, J.B., & Ann Miner (1992). "The Shadow of the Future: Effects of Anticipated Interaction and Frequency of Contact on Buyer-Seller Cooperation." *Academy of Management Journal* 35, no. 2: 265–291.

29. Author interview, November 19, 1996.

30. Malinowski, B. (1932). *Argonauts of the Western Pacific.* London: Routledge & Kegan Paul; Mauss, M. (1967). *The Gift: Forms and Functions of Exchange in Archaic Societies.* New York: Norton; Gouldner, A.W. (1960). "The Norm of Reciprocity: A Preliminary Statement." *American Sociological Review* 25, no. 1: 161–178.

31. Gouldner, "The Norm of Reciprocity."

32. See Ouchi, W. (1981) *Theory Z.* Reading, Mass.: Addison-Wesley; Fruin, W. M. (1992). *The Japanese Enterprise System.* New York: Oxford University Press.

33. Helper, S., & M. Sako (1995). "Supplier Relations in Japan and the United States: Are They Converging?" *Sloan Management Review* (spring): 77–84.

34. Cusumano, M. (1985). *The Japanese Automobile Industry: Technology and Management at Nissan and Toyota.* Cambridge, Mass.: The Council on East Asian Studies, Harvard University.

Chapter 5

Epigraph source: *Business Week* (January 27, 1992).

1. Author interview, March 1992.

2. Author interview, April 1992.

3. Author interview, December 11, 1995.

4. Author interview, September 14, 1995.

5. Author Interview, October 1994.

6. Author interview, September 24, 1995.

7. Author interview, October 22, 1996.

8. Author Interview, October 1994.

9. Author Interview, March 1997.

10. Rommel, G.K., R.D. Kempis, & H.W. Kaas (1994). "Does Quality Pay?" *McKinsey Quarterly,* no. 1: 51–63.

11. Author Interview, October 1994.

12. Helper, S. (1991). "How Much has Really Changed Between U.S. Automakers and Their Suppliers?" *Sloan Management Review* (summer).

13. Author Interview, June 1995.

14. Author Interview, October 1994.

15. Author Interview, October 1994.

16. Author Interview, December 1995.

17. Author Interview, April 1994.

Chapter 6

Epigraph source: *Automotive Industries* (April 1994): 60.

1. *Automotive Industries* (February 1996): 79.

2. Author interview, July 7, 1997; Author interview, April 14, 1997.

3. Author interview, April 24, 1994.

4. Author interview, April 25, 1994.

5. Author interview, October 25, 1995.

6. Author interview, March 10, 1994.

7. Author interview, March 10, 1994.

8. Author interview, April 25, 1994.

9. Ingrassia and White (1994). *Comeback: The Fall & Rise of the American Automobile Industry*. New York: Simon and Schuster.

10. "Following Chrysler" (1994). *The Economist* (April 23): 66–67.

11. Author interview, June 9, 1994.

12. Ghemawat, P. (1986). "Sustainable Advantage." *Harvard Business Review*. (September/October).

13. Author interview, November 11, 1995.

14. Walton, M. (1986). *The Deming Management Method*. New York: Pedigree Books.

15. Clark, K.B., & T. Fujimoto (1991). *Product Development Performance*. Boston: Harvard Business School Press, p. 40.

16. Stalk, G., & T.M. Hout (1990). *Competing Against Time*. New York: The Free Press; Clark & Fujimoto, *Product Development Performance*, p. 40.

17. Author interview, November 11, 1995.

18. J.D. Power and Associates, 1990 and 1997 Initial Quality Surveys.

Chapter 7

Epigraph source: Author interview, June 11, 1996.

1. Kogut B., & U. Zander (1992). "Knowledge of the Firm, Combinative Capabilities, and the Replication of Technology." *Organization Science* 3, no. 3: 383–397.

2. MacDuffie J.P., & S. Helper (1998). *California Management Review*.

3. Kogut B., & U. Zander (1996). "What Firms Do? Coordination, Identity, and Learning." *Organization Science* 7, no. 5: 502–503.

4. Kogut, B. (1999). "The Network as Knowledge." *Strategic Management Journal*, special issue, conference, Northwestern University, April.

5. Author interview with Koichiro Noguchi, August 1993.

6. Author interview, June 1996.

7. Then GM President Charles Wilson, quoted in *The New York Times*, November 9, 1992, made these remarks in 1953.

8. Author Interview, January 1997.

9. Author interview, November 17, 1997.

10. Author interview, November 18, 1997.

11. Author Interview, November 19, 1996.

12. Author interview, November 1996.
13. Author interview, November 1997.
14. Author interview, November 1996.

Conclusion

Epigraph source: Magretta, J. (1998) "The power of virtual integration: An interview with Dell Computer's Michael Dell." *Harvard Business Review* (March-April): 75.
Epigraph source: A Chrysler executive told me that Lutz used this phrase, November 11, 1995.

1. Baldwin & Clark (1997).
2. *Detroit News* (July 10, 1998).
3. *Automotive Industries* (February 1996).
4. *Industry Week* (March 17, 1997).
5. *Automotive News* (June 9, 1997).
6. *Industry Week* (March 17, 1997).
7. *Automotive News* (June 9, 1997): 3.
8. Nishiguchi, T., & M. Fruin (1993). "Supplying the Toyota Production System: Intercorporate Evolution and Supplier Subsystems." In *Country Competitiveness*, ed. B. Kogut. New York: Oxford University Press.
9. Author interview, July 1993.
10. Internal Chrysler document, 1996.
11. Internal Chrysler document, 1996.
12. Author Interview, July 1998.
13. Author Interview, July 1998.
14. Author Interview, February 8, 2000.
15. Kelly, K. (1998). *New Rules for the New Economy.* New York: Penguin Books, p. 26.
16. Porter, M.E. (1980). *Competitive Strategy.* New York: The Free Press, p. 123.
17. Author Interview, October 1996.

Index

Automotive Industries, 133
Automotive News, 134

Badaracco, Joseph, Jr., 28–29
Bain and Co., viii, 145
BAMA. *See* Bluegrass Automotive
   Manufacturers Association
Barretti, Roberto, 174
Bedard, Bernie, 137
Bidding auctions, online, for non-
   strategic inputs, 156
Blown to Bits (Evans and Wurster), 5
Bluegrass Automotive Manufac-
   turers Association (BAMA), 65,
   73, 163–164
Borlem SA, 172
Brice, John, 128
Bridgestone, Inc., 152, 172
Brooks, David, 6, 17, 60

CAD/CAM (Computer Aided
   Design/Computer Aided Manufacturing software), Chrysler
   suppliers and, 129
California Management Review, 11
Capabilities benchmarking, in
   supplier selection, 155
Castaing, François, 114, 116, 117,
   124–125, 126
CATIA (Computer Aided
   Design/Computer Aided Manufacturing software), 129
Change, by suppliers, liability and,
   84–85
Chrysler. *See also* Daimler-Chrysler
   in 1980s, viii–ix, 5–6, 6, 114–117
   and AMC acquisition, 115–116
   Daimler-Benz merger, 20–22,
   178–180

development of new products, 6,
   113–122, 134–141, *137*
employment tenure at, 106, 141
as extended enterprise, 10,
   130–131, 147–148, 160–162,
   178–180
governance profile, 34
inventory levels, and supplier
   proximity, 44–45, *44*
knowledge sharing at, 90t, 96–97,
   96, 117, 118t, 123–130. *See also*
   Supplier Cost Reduction Effort
   (SCORE)
LH program, 116–117, 118t,
   121–122, 124, 138–139
market share, reorganization
   and, 146, *147*
and Mitsubishi, joint venture
   with, 117
and modularization, 172
parts division, labor costs, 56
and production, cost savings in,
   141–143
profits, 8, *9*, 113–114, 116, 133, 146,
   147, 183
quality control, 145–146, *145*
reorganization of
   and communication, 120
   and competitiveness, 6–7
   and Honda, as model, 114–115
   and *Keiretsu* model, 113–117,
   130–131, 132
   and market share, 146, *147*
   and new product development, 119, 121–122
   and pre-sourcing, 120–121
   and profits, 133, 146, *147*
   success of, vii, viii, 5, 9, 10,
   130–134, 148–149

in supplier selection process,
101–103, *103*, 155
at Toyota, 90–91, 90t, 94–100,
93–96, 105–106, 108–109,
164–168, *166*
and transaction costs, 91–96,
93–95, 108
U.S. automakers and, 123
TRW Corp., 177
TSSC. *See* Toyota Supplier Support
Center

Union Mantein, 172
United States, 62, *62*, 162–167

Valade, Gary, 21
Value-added partnerships, defini-
tion of, 27
Value chain, definition of, 5. *See also*
Extended enterprise(s)
VDO Kinzie Comercio *e* Servicos,
172
Vertical integration

advantages and disadvantages of,
53–56
at Chrysler, 34
contemporary value of, 26
definition of, 24
at Ford, *33*, 34–35
at GM, *33*, 34–35
guidelines for, 19–20, 24–26
in Japanese firms, 35–36
shift away from, 171
at Toyota, 13, 33 f, 34
trends disfavoring, 27–31, *27*
Virtual corporations. *See* Extended
enterprise(s)
Virtual integration, 26
Volkswagen, 172–174
Volvo, 36

Womack, James, 10
Wurster, Thomas S., 5

Zimmer, Steve, 132

Printed in the United States
95523LV00004B/180/A